CONFESSIONS

of a

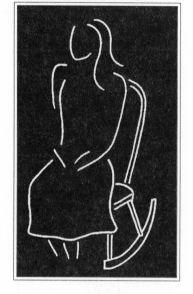

LOST

MOTHER

by

ElisaMB@aol.com

D1379753

GATEWAY PRESS, INC.
Baltimore, MD   1996

Front cover illustration by Bruce Rydell
Back cover photograph by Zoë Barton

Permissions:
Gorka, John, lyrics to "Good Noise," from the album *Out of the Valley.* Windham Hill Records, Fleming, Tamulevich & Associates, 1994.

Page, Jimmy and Plant, Robert, lyrics to "Stairway to Heaven" from the album *Led Zeppelin.* Atlantic Recording Corporation, Warner Communications Company. 1971.

Waldron, Jan, *Giving Away Simone*, pp. xvi, xvii. New York: Times Books, 1995.

Library of Congress Cataloging in Publication Data
        Barton, Elisa M.
        Confessions of a Lost Mother
        p. cm.
        1. Barton, Elisa M. —Correspondence. 2. Birthmothers—United States—Correspondence. 3. Adoptees—United States—Identification——Case Studies. 4. Adoption—United States—Psychological aspects——Case Studies. 5. Internet (Computer network) 6. Mailing lists.
I. Title.
HV874.82.B38A3   1996
362.82'96'092--dc20
ISBN 0-9650795-0-3

Direct all correspondence and book orders to:
E. M. Barton
744 Clarendon Road
Narberth, PA 19072-1519
e-mail address: menocal@aol.com

Typesetting by The Letter Edge

Published for the author by
Gateway Press, Inc.
1001 N. Calvert Street
Baltimore, MD 21202

Printed in the United States of America

@ **Contents** @

Foreword v

Acknowledgments vii

Prologue ix

A Preview of My E-mail Correspondents xv

Chapter One 1

Bless me, Father, for I have sinned . . .

@ Open Letter to Adoptees @ Confession & Apology @ The Transition
@ The Leap Year Father @ Regrets @ "Return to Sender" @

Chapter Two 31

Stairway to Heaven

@ *Stairway to Heaven* lyrics by Led Zeppelin, 1971 @ Pounded in the Fire
@ That Little Bracelet @ Finding Anna; Reply @ Orphan Voyages @
Post-Traumatic Adoption Syndrome @ E.R. @ Unconditional Love @
The Empty Limbs of the Family Tree @ "Birthmother's Choice" @ Head
vs. Heart @ The Timebomb Theory @ Find Your Daughter @ Why
Search? @ Contacting Minors Directly @ A Time and Place @
Beethoven's Eighteenth Symphony @ Break on Through @ Stairway to
Heaven @

Chapter Three **75**

Who Is My Mother? And Who Are My Siblings?

@ Animal Adoption @ "Are You My Daddy?" @ Rejection, Secrecy, Survival @ The Smell of Belonging @ Synchronicity @ Mother of Three @ My Mother Liked to Tap Dance; Reply @ Today My Mother Became Real; Reply @ An Adoptee's Impossible Dream @ Breaking the Iceberg @ Danya's "Sperm Donor" @ Call Me "Mom" @ The Original Unmother @ My Children's Mothers @ Turtle Soup @ Scarred for Life @ Hibernation @

Chapter Four **111**

Make a Good Noise

@ *Good Noise*, lyrics by John Gorka, 1994. @ Oxygen Mask @ The Birds, the Bees, and Relinquishment @ Coercion @ Open Letter to Adoptive Parents @ Denial and Healing @ Cat's Lament: An Adoptee Speaks Out @ Abortion and Adoption @ The Question Birthmothers Were Not Asked @ In Whose Best Interests? @ Single Motherhood in Germany @ Twenty-Six-Year-Old Memories @ Birthfathers Have Secrets, Too @ Out of the Birthmother Closet @ The Only One @ The Best Adoption Whorehouse in America @ Elephant in the Living Room @ Firetruck in the Living Room @ Christopher's Story @ The Electric Koolaid Adoption Test @ La Cocotte-Minute @ A New Question from an Old Friend @ Everybirthparent @

@ **Foreword** @

An anonymous soul once observed that it is easier to understand a nation by listening to its music than by learning its language. Upon my first reading of *Confessions of a Lost Mother*, it struck me that by weaving together her own story with those of others, Elisa Barton has written a song: a song of birthmothers. One must listen to it closely to begin to understand the impact adoption has had upon their lives.

I was introduced to Elisa by Annette Baran over a late-afternoon glass of wine at the annual CERA conference in the autumn of 1995. With passionate zeal, Elisa shared that she wanted to publish a book of electronic mail correspondence between birthmothers and other triad members. Unique ideas are rare—I had never heard of a book based upon cyberspace communication, and, indeed, *Confessions* may be the first. That afternoon, although Elisa sought encouragement and guidance, she needed neither. It was imperative to her that she get this book into print, and the fact that her manuscript was ready for the printer a mere four months later is a testament to her personal commitment and resolve.

The perspectives within *Confessions* are a different 'music' than my own. As an adoptee, I've generally felt I entered adoption as a passive participant. Hence, I have not had to anguish over choices made, over advice heeded, or over submission to coercion. My 'timebombs' and struggles are not the same as a birthmother's—which is exactly why *Confessions* is of enormous value to me. It is important for triad members to communicate and understand the experience and need of each other, and for society as a whole to try to understand the lifelong turmoil that adoption can cause. Such enlightenment occurs when one is able to 'step momentarily into the shoes of another.' Elisa provides that experience through her powerful, intimate narrative and a chorus of other voices.

As we stand on the brink of new legislation and a new millennium, it is the collective experiences of those whose lives have been affected by adoption which should guide future adoption policy. Books like *Confessions* help provide an anthology of triad voices from which others can learn. As Thoreau once remarked, "A book should contain pure discoveries, glimpses of terra firma, though by shipwrecked mariners— not the art of navigation by those who have never been out of sight of land."

Confessions leads us into the often painful terra firma where birthmothers, and others affected by adoption, reside. Listen to the music.

Jean A. S. Strauss, author of
The Great Adoptee Searchbook and
Birthright: The Guide to Search and Reunion
January 31, 1996

@ **Acknowledgments** @

I am especially indebted to all of the Internet correspondents who generously gave permission to include portions of their e-mail letters and posts.

I gratefully acknowledge the many friends and family members, both on-line and off-line, without whose gifts of encouragement these pages would never have left cyberspace:

My husband; our four little women; my parents and siblings, for their abiding love and understanding. L. Anne Babb, Amy Bergman, Andi Finnegan, Andrew Katz, Alicia Lanier, Laura Lewis, Diane Ortery, and Elizabeth Walker, for making me write before I thought. Margret Barner, for corresponding with me in German. Joy Renjilian-Burgy, for listening, always. Vicki Camp, Tony LeClerc, Susan Friel-Williams, and Sharon Robinson, for their warm embraces when I most needed them. Elizabeth Carroll, for the love of her adopted children. Julie Bailey, Melinda Corday, Kate Davey, Steve Lustgarten, Jarrett Kroll, Billie McCabe, Dorene Morin, Lisa Qualls, Michele Rice, Janet Bray Solursh, Judy Sullivan, Becky Wheeler and Curry Wolfe, for making me think before I wrote. Annette Baran, for sharing her wisdom and her warmth. C. Bertram, for her unmitigated truthfulness. Beki Brindle-DeMyer, for the love of her son. Nathan Brindle, for the love of his sister Beki. Paul Broholm, Ann Craig and Russell Heath, for their true-blue friendship. Yvette Carter, for the love of her sisters-in-adoption. Mary Anne Manning Cohen, for telling me to "learn the difference between giving advice and giving orders." Rebecca Dalton and Teri Liston, for sending me their hearts and diskettes of my posts. Ann Hughes, for becoming my friend and my publisher. Heidi Hiemstra, for her inspiringly sincere questions. Stacy Kludt, for her abiding encouragement. Margy McMorrow, for her sweet Irish temper. Michael Parker, for opening his heart to fear. Kirby Pierce, for the love of his lost mother. Joan Poppers, for being my best friend in cyberspace. Clayton Shaw, for his wonderful editorial and marketing ideas. Jean Strauss, for convincing me to self-publish.

I have undoubtedly left out several names. Please forgive me if I have forgotten to include yours. You know who you are.

Elisa Menocal Barton

@ **Prologue** @

"What was it like, giving up a child?"

That question now stunned and stung me like no other. Not once had my sister or my mother, my spouse or my friend, a social worker, psychiatrist or marriage counselor, a pastor or a priest, put that question to me.

I had never hidden the fact of my out-of-wedlock pregnancy. I was twenty years old. I had just returned to college after a year of study abroad. A nurse at Student Health Services informed me that I was carrying a twelve-week-old fetus. Seven months later, I gave birth to a baby boy. I signed the surrender papers seventy-two hours after birth. Ten months after that, on Commencement Day, I exchanged a black cap and gown for a white bridal costume.

Here, nearly twenty years later, was the essential question. But I could not see the questioner's face. I could not hear the intonation of her voice. The question was staring at me from my computer screen. It was the voice of a young adopted woman, seeking the answers to her own sense of abandonment and bewilderment. I instinctively recognized that question to be at the core of my own shrouded grief.

As I sought to answer the question for the adoptee, a mystery began to unravel. Long-buried feelings of bitterness and betrayal, of sorrow and resentment, gradually began to surface. Although I had busied myself raising four delightful daughters and building a career, it was as if I had just emerged from a deep emotional freeze. Memories and feelings began to spill out as if I had just swallowed a near-overdose of truth serum!

Although I had long since searched for and located my relinquished son, I had only just begun to mourn the loss of my firstborn child. My fingers did the crying, through the *Internet Yellow Pages*.

Jan Waldron's prosaic memoir *Giving Away Simone* (New York: Times Books, 1995) accurately states the following statistics: "There are approximately 6 million adoptees in the United States. By extension, there are 12 million birthparents and 12 million adoptive parents—30 million people directly involved in adoption. Add to that number the untraceable millions of other birth and adoptive relations, and the percentage of our population touched by the act of adoption grows beyond imagination . . ." (page xvi)

Waldron also underlines the importance behind the publication of memoirs such as ours: "The upside of the current confessional climate in this country . . . is the undoing of a conspiracy to erase ourselves and the effort to give life to the stories we've been expected to hide. (There are millions of birthmothers in this country, yet most people will tell you they've never met one. Nearly as many will tell you they don't know what one is.)" (page xvii).

On his computer, my husband had read about an "Internet mailing list" for women who had surrendered a child to adoption. He had correctly sensed that I might be interested in this on-line support group. I understood that it had something to do with e-mail, about which I had not a clue. I hastily jotted down a message for my husband to send to the lady in charge: "I am the birth mother of a teenage son. Please add me to your mailing list."

The following day, my husband yelled upstairs from his office, "Hey, Elisa! You've got e-mail!" He transferred the e-mail letters onto a disk for me. I put the disk into my own Macintosh computer and *voila*! I beheld my first electronic posts! They looked weird. For some odd reason, the messages alternated between full-length and one-word lines. At the top and bottom there were indecipherable codes of letters and digits, "REs," "headers," things between and semi-colons and :). I was perplexed by the form but enchanted by the content.

By taking this one small step into cyberspace, I inadvertently took a giant leap into an e-mail confessional where the universal language of truth was spoken! Despite our diverse religious, cultural, or academic backgrounds, we each shared an intimate and often painful connection to adoption.

The Internet mailing lists mentioned here are support and discussion groups. While they are not on-line search organizations or reunion registries, they do comprise many resourceful and helpful individuals. A mailing list is a live global support network made up of many invisible but active listeners. Mailing lists function in ways similar to magazine or newsletter subscriptions, with two important distinctions: 1. Each subscriber determines his or her own quantity and quality of editing and "posting" (Internetese for publishing) 2. List mail is spontaneously generated around the clock and around the world! Any post which is addressed to the mailing list is automatically and instantly e-mailed to each and every other subscriber.

The unique subscription policies of a mailing list are determined by, and often reflect, the personal philosophy of its original founder. For example, there is a mailing list for adoptees only; another for birthmothers only; yet another for any member of the adoption triad. There is excellent cooperation, collaboration and communication between each of these on-line groups. Many individuals subscribe to more than one mailing list.

Confessions of a Lost Mother comprises two types of Internet communications:

1. Posts to an Internet mailing list. For example,

> Subject: Open Letter to Adoptees
> Date: 6 July 23:15 EDT
> From: ElisaMB@aol.com
> To: Adoption Triad Mailing List

2. E-mail letters between myself and my personal correspondents. For example,

> Subject: Re: Finding Anna
> Date: June 11 18:44:26 PM EST
> From: DJ@aol.com
> To: ElisaMB@aol.com

The names and e-mail addresses of most correspondents, family members, friends, and Internet mailing lists have been altered to protect their privacy. Pseudonyms are marked with an asterisk (*) at first mention in the text. The letter "headers" (dates and times at which they were originally posted) are authentic. Some of the original subject titles have been changed.

Internet addresses change too often to make any specific listings practical. Private e-mail addresses are like unlisted telephone numbers, to be shared only with those whom one trusts. Up-to-date and accurate public Internet resources and e-mail addresses, such as the adoption-related mailing lists, are available through the larger commercial mail services (*America Online, Prodigy, Compuserve, Delphi*, etc.) Each of these Internet services sponsors its own adoption-related message boards and forums. Some hold regularly-scheduled "live chats" for adoption-triad members. The Adoption Forum of America Online also maintains a search registry which has facilitated many online reunions.

What began as mere words on a computer screen ultimately became the caring voices, faces, and spirit of true human interaction. Within weeks of receiving my first e-mail letter from another birthmother, I found myself in daily, sometimes hourly, electronic correspondence with hundreds of women and men of all ages, from around the globe. Inspired by their persistent honesty and warmth, I began to relate my own story. Every day I would meet a new mother, father, son, daughter, or sibling who was seeking a lost family member. Many others had already found their loved ones, but were now struggling with the consequences of a long and difficult separation. I soon discovered that I was not the only person whose spirit and heart felt broken. Unwittingly, I embarked on a cyberspacious journey to mend them both.

While that journey is far from concluded, the time felt ripe to render *Confessions of a Lost Mother* into the more traditional and accessible format of the printed page. As I have told the e-mail correspondents whom you are about to meet, getting this book into print feels like giving birth to an overdue baby! Celebrate with me now as the long-lost becomes newly found.

@ A Preview of My E-mail Correspondents @

Alicia@aol.com (Birth mother, Texas): I continue to write and to make presentations about issues affecting women who relinquished in an era of adoption secrecy; and about the practical and emotional issues experienced by all others who are touched by adoption. I use the Internet in my efforts to encourage more enlightened adoption legislation, including giving adoptees access to their original birth records.

Celeste@eeyore.com (Birth mother, Minnesota): The subject of adoption is like a magnet to me. It attracts me like no other, but it can also repel me, like some familiar yet foreign element. I found my birthson two-and-a-half years ago. At this date, he is not ready for a relationship. I remain "expectant."

Danya@american.edu (Adoptee, Washington, D.C.): Due entirely to my access to the Internet, and to all of its practical and emotional resources, I have now been successfully reunited for four months! When I was delaying the final step of my search for my birth mother, because I was emotionally upset and confused and worried that contact would make things worse, Elisa's suggestion that things couldn't get much worse convinced me to proceed!

Janet@uga.edu (Adoptee, Georgia): I got married on Sunday. My birthfamily was represented by my mother's youngest brother, a policeman in my hometown. He came with his wife, and they sat with my adoptive cousins. My birth-grandparents and my birth-aunt sent very sweet and touching cards and substantial cash gifts. I wish that my birth mom could have been there.

Joan@aol.com (Birth mother, California): Moving towards the two-year mark of reunion, it still amazes me that my daughter is back in my life. I still get goose bumps when I recall the conversation with Tony from International Soundex Reunion Registry saying, "We have a match!" I don't know if I will ever be free of the pain of those lost years, but I treasure the opportunity I have now, of building a new life with my daughter. I wonder if I will ever look at her without staring in awe. I hope not.

Judy@uvm.edu (Birth mother, Vermont): Finding my son has changed my life forever. Society had shunned my pregnancy, calling me "bad" because my choices had led to the birth of an illegitimate child. Reunion has helped to seal a wound which festered for over a quarter century. No measure of happiness compares to finally knowing my son's name, hearing his voice, and seeing him in person. He could finally receive his heritage and stop wondering about his roots. Love has prevailed in the face of adversity and scorn, from a society that was less than kind.

Kate@dartmouth.edu (Birth mother, New Hampshire): Finding my daughter, I have discovered more of myself. After our first conversation on the telephone, I was at once elated, but also faced with the realization that life, although now infinitely more rich, did not suddenly become easier. The search continues, as we have yet to meet in person; the struggle continues; the journey continues. Reunion is not a point in time. It is another phase in the process of learning, healing, and understanding who we are.

Larina@world.com (Birth mother and adoptee, Massachusetts): When my daughter turned three years old, she and her adoptive mom called me on the phone. I treasure the little voice on my answering machine saying, "I love you." The openness in my adoption plan went from total control to complete loss of control over the welfare of my baby. We fortunately chose adoptive parents who are genuine in their desire for openness. Regular phone calls and photographs have helped my heart to heal. The birthfather and I are debating the costs, emotionally and otherwise, of bearing another child. I am more sure of my abilities to parent now.

Michele@aol.com (Birth mother, Colorado): When my son Greg "found" me in October of 1994, I realized instantly that I had a lot of work to do to get ready for our meeting seven weeks later. I needed to reach that scared, vulnerable seventeen-year-old girl, to hate her and then to forgive her. I have lost twenty-five pounds, shedding twenty-five years of tears. I have more energy. I look five years younger. Greg and I are enjoying a wonderful reunion. The future is brighter for both of us.

Mimi@aol.com (Adoptive mother, Minnesota): My Internet and on-line friendships have allowed me to better understand what adoption has meant from the perspective of my adopted children's other mothers. I have been challenged to face and to work through many of my fears. I never believed the lie that birth mothers are able to easily get on with their lives. If I had placed a baby for adoption, no power on earth would keep me from searching. Birth and adoption records must be unsealed.

CHAPTER ONE

Bless me, Father, for I have sinned ...

@ *Open Letter to Adoptees* @

Date: 6 July 23:15 EDT
From: ElisaMB@aol.com
To: Adoption Triad Mailing List

Janet wrote: « I don't know if the adoption was coerced, if my birth mother would have preferred an abortion but was genuinely frightened of taking her life in her hands, or if she was that touted ideal of the caring, giving, selfless mother who gave me up because she couldn't care for me. After listening to the women here talk about their experiences, I can't believe that this touted ideal exists outside of the pretty fantasies of adoptive parents and legislators. »

I was twenty-one and a college undergraduate when I gave birth to my firstborn child. You've spent most of your life imagining who your original parents are; I've spent many years imagining the life of my son.

Throughout these years, I've met hundreds of women who, like myself, felt they had no choice but to surrender their child for adoption. That includes women who surrendered their child for some of the reasons you may have suspected: abandonment by the baby's father; rape; drug or alcohol dependency. By and large, however, women who have lost a child to adoption have done so for lack of social, emotional, and financial support. The great majority did everything within their limited power to keep their children. I know of

several instances where the adoption was not only psychologically but, indeed, physically coerced.

I have never met a woman who threw her baby in a dump-
ster, although I understand that this story is the kind which
the media is most likely to report. I have never met a woman
who gave up her baby because she found it ugly at birth, as
an adopted college student of mine suspected about his own
birth mother. I don't know any "whores" (another fantasy of
my student) who lost their babies to adoption. Most are women
who were in love with the father of their firstborn child.

I have met a lot of birth fathers as well. They are not generally
rapists. Many were never told that they were fathers until
after the adoption placement. Many were young guys who
were as ignorant, scared, and as lacking in support as their
pregnant girlfriends.

Between the time of surrender and reunion, birth parents
often have the same kind of nightmare fantasies about their
children as many adoptees have expressed having about their
birth parents. The worst, and most common nightmare, is
that her child will have been abused or murdered by its adoptive parents. For the mother of Lisa Steinberg, this nightmare
became a reality. Other fears include not finding one's child
alive or "normal" for any other reason. Numerous adoptees
and birth parents have died before being reunited. I am personally acquainted with three mothers whose surrendered
children have taken their own lives. Two of these mothers
searched for their teenage sons, only to find that they had
committed suicide several months earlier.

Most birth mothers and birth fathers have about as accurate
an idea of how the surrender will affect the rest of their lives
as do the adoptees. In whichever year your mother gave birth
to you, she was undoubtedly told by the adoption agency (as

well as by clergy, lawyers, doctors, parents, friends) that she would eventually marry, have other children, put all of this behind her, get on with her life, etc. As the birth mother often has never experienced marriage or mothering before, she has no choice but to believe that this may be true. (And it is entirely false. I'll discuss the "post-traumatic birth mother syndrome" in another post.) She was probably also told that it would be selfish to keep you and raise you as a single mother, when there were "so many more deserving and infertile adoptive couples waiting to love and legitimize" you. A healthy white newborn was then, and still is, a highly prized acquisition. This does not mean that you may have been sold on the black market. It means that your mother may have been as great a casualty of your adoption as you were.

But mothers who have relinquished their children to adoption are further condemned to feel shameful to even admit it or to speak about it. To a great degree, I am still reluctant to share the details of this very painful part of my life for fear of being judged by some or of offending others.

I am presently a foreign language teacher and film translator. I have been married for nearly twenty years. My husband and I are raising four daughters. My son *Jacob is almost eighteen, but he has the mind of a younger child. I was unaware of his handicaps until I found him a few years ago.

*Danya asked, «What was it like, giving up a child?» Even in the semi-anonymous and relatively impersonal format of this Internet forum, to answer that question honestly would be painful. I will try to answer it at some later date.

In the meantime, I'd like to hear more about why you adoptees think (or thought) that you were given up for adoption, before having heard the truth from your birth parent.

@ *Confession & Apology* @

Date: 19 July 09:48:09 PDT
From: ElisaMB@aol.com
To: *bmoms@abcd.edu

I have a confession and a public apology to make.

My husband and I had just moved to Cambridge, Massachusetts after the wedding. I was desperate to have another baby right away. My husband wanted to wait at least a year before conceiving our first child. Throughout that first year of waiting, it felt like I was treading water . . . and just barely keeping my head above ever-deepening black waves.

That first honeymoon summer, my husband read an ad on his daily commuter metro to work, about a group called Birthright of Greater Boston. He suggested that I might make a good volunteer counselor.

Birthright is a non-profit counseling center for women in crisis pregnancies. It is basically a pro-life group. They are interested in saving babies from being aborted. Beyond that, they would help the mother with whatever decision she made, whether it was to keep the baby or to place it for adoption. My volunteer work, helping resourceless mothers-to-be, began as a personal catharsis. I didn't realize until much later that it was like the blind leading the blind.

One day at the Birthright office, I got a call from a woman who said she was a birth mother and that there was a support group called Concerned United Birthparents. Their meetings were held at Park Street Church, right around the corner from the Birthright office. Gail was surprised to find that Birthright had an actual birth mother on their staff. She promptly invited me to come to the next C.U.B. meeting. I asked her what they did. She said that they were all birth mothers learning to cope with the pain of having lost their children to adoption. I was O.K. with that. Gail added that she had just searched for and found her nine-year-old daughter. I remember thinking to myself, "Oh, no. I could not deal with this for another decade! This woman must be crazy. Why can't she just cut the apron strings and let go?"

I said nothing to Gail. I never went to that or to any other C.U.B. meeting in the Boston area. I was convinced that these women, especially the ones who decided to search for their young children, were just creating and prolonging their own misery. I believed that my own pain would go away, just as soon as I gave birth to, and kept, my own "first" baby.

Over the next three years, I concentrated on just that. I gave birth to my first, then my second, then my third daughter. I continued to work as a volunteer counselor for Birthright the entire time. I networked with every maternity ward, social service agency, and adoption agency in and around Boston, trying to help the women and girls considering adoption for their babies. If and when a prospective birth mother asked me about my own experience, I would say, "As you can see, I am now married and I have my own babies. It has worked out just fine for me."

I pray to God that those two or three women for whom I held myself as a shining example of birthmother-sainthood will forgive me, but I wouldn't blame them if they have since condemned me to hell.

@ *The Transition* @

Date: 21 July 08:02:36 PDT
From: ElisaMB@aol.com
To: bmoms@abcd.edu

Why did I stop advising unwed mothers to relinquish their babies for adoption? Why did I begin to encourage other birth mothers to search for their lost babies, as soon as they felt able and willing? The transition occurred quite gradually, over a period of fifteen years. If I had been keeping a journal, it would have read as follows:

Mother's Day, 1979: The baby I've lost to adoption is not quite three years old. *Preston and I are about to celebrate our second anniversary with our own baby! Finally, I have my own infant to love and to hold. I feel relieved that I have not given birth to another baby boy. But why am I rocking this child and crying all the time?

Thanksgiving, 1980: *Chloe is only nineteen months old when our second daughter, *Leigh, is born. Now I am rocking two babies and crying.

January, 1981: There's a Phil Donohue show with a tall blond woman whose name I vaguely recall. Oh! It's the woman who began that group called Concerned United Birthparents in 1976, the year I gave my baby boy up for adoption. A mother-daughter reunion takes place right on the air! Both women are overweight and have the same ecstatic teary smiles on their faces. They are locked in a hysterical embrace. Lee Campbell answers questions from the studio audience about adoption, about birth mothers and about reunions. She says that 95% of all birth mothers want to be reunited with their lost children.

The day after the Phil Donohue show, I decide to write my first letter to my baby's adoptive parents. I send a picture of myself holding both of my baby daughters. I update them on my life since I last saw my son in the hospital. I send the letter to the adoption agency and ask them to please forward it to my baby's new family.

September, 1981: I've begun teaching Spanish part-time at Boston College. I explain the verb *gatear* (from *gato*, it means "to crawl") using Leigh as my favorite example. Crawling babies do kind of look like cats. Chloe is a beautiful, timid, curly-headed little creature. My students are mostly Catholic, white, and from hard-working blue-collar families. A number of the girls offer to baby-sit.

Thanksgiving, 1981: I've been waiting since January to hear back from either the adoptive parents or from the agency. Nothing. I write to the agency once again and ask whether they ever received the letter. No reply, so I call them. The social worker explains that my letter had contained "identifying information," which, by law, they could not forward to the adoptive parents. They had put the letter in my file, for my son, "if he should ever decide to come looking for it once he becomes an adult."

It angers me that the agency has let all these months go by without telling me this. I write again to ask if they would forward a different letter to the adoptive family, one without any "identifying information."

February, 1982: In Spanish class today, my students had a debate about abortion. The issues of premarital sex and unwed parenthood came up. The students wanted to know my personal opinions. I dared not confess to them that I had given up a baby for adoption.

March, 1982: Since I began teaching again, I have been working at the Birthright office less, usually one or two Saturday mornings per month. This Saturday morning I go to the Birthright office and perform yet another of the urine-analysis pregnancy tests. It is positive. This time, the results are my own.

April, 1982: One of my former Birthright clients, *Janice, has become my closest friend. She had aborted her first unplanned pregnancy and came to the Birthright office for help when she became pregnant a second time. The father *William, who is younger than Janice, was scared about becoming a father, and about committing to marriage. Janice thinks I have helped her to avoid having another abortion, but it is she who has taught me much about the viability of single parenting. Their joyous wedding celebration has finally taken place. Their three-year-old son was the ring-bearer.

June and July, 1982: It looks like I won't be teaching next fall, what with two pre-schoolers and another baby due in November. So I have begun to help out a bit more with Birthright again. Adoption agencies are inviting me to come and speak to prospective adoptive parents. Maternity homes want me to come and speak to their unwed mothers-to-be. They all want to use me as an example of a mother who made the right choice.

I am counseling two young women right now. They each want me to attend their births. Why do I have so many conflicting feelings? I am not able to attend the first of these two births. The young mother has become a friend of sorts. *Sherry has been to my house. She has met my husband and my two little girls. She has been asking many questions about what it feels like after the baby is gone. She is using the adoption agency I recommended to her as the best I could find in Boston. I have advised her, as I was once advised, that it is probably not a great idea for her to breast-feed the baby, but that she could try expressing the colostrum into a bottle. I go to visit mother and baby at the hospital. She is breast-feeding the baby. She is sobbing. I wish I could tell her to change the damned "adoption plan," take the baby and run! But I don't. Sherry is discharged from the hospital without her infant son.

I get a call late at night from the other expectant mother. *Kristin has wavered throughout her pregnancy over whether to keep the baby or to place it for adoption. She, too, has met my husband and two little girls, and asked me lots of questions about losing a baby to adoption. Our pregnancies have overlapped by a few months. She is in labor now, and she wants me to be there with her. I meet her at Brigham and Women's Hospital. They have just begun to induce her. Thank God, they also give her an epidural. I take turns with the labor and delivery nurses, supporting her through the long night. She finally delivers a beautiful baby girl. Kristin names her baby *Adrienne.

After a few days, mother and daughter leave the hospital together. I quickly gather new and donated baby clothes and furniture for her, and make my husband transport it to Kristin's dingy apartment in Brighton. I tell Kristin to call me anytime, but it hurts me to see her with her baby. Maybe Kristin senses this. Over the remainder of the summer, I do not hear much from her. Instead, she takes my advice to develop a new support network for herself.

I call Sherry and ask how she is doing. She doesn't have much to say to me, either.

August, 1982: A local cable television station has asked the director of Birthright to do a short live segment. He has asked me to go on the air with him. He has brought the models of a developing fetus which we use in the Birthright office. I pick up the six-month-old fetus and hold it in front of my early third trimester pregnant bulge. "Here's what my baby looks like in there right now," I say on television. There is no VCR to tape the show, but my friend Janice later calls me in hysterics, telling me she saw me holding that ridiculous plastic baby in front of my bulging stomach. Janice is six months pregnant, too.

September, 1982: At the ladies' bible study which Janice and I attend together on Thursday mornings at my church in Newton, we run into Kristin and Adrienne for the first time since delivering the layette. My toddler daughters Chloe and Leigh love the baby and want to fondle her. Kristin looks tired and scared but there is a genuine smile of pride and a sense of peace emanating from her as she holds Adrienne. Do I dare acknowledge to myself that those feelings have now eluded me three times?

November, 1982: My third baby girl is born. I name her *Suzanne. My husband says she looks just like my father. She looks a lot like her unnamed brother. My good friend Janice has also just given birth to William's second child, a beautiful daughter. I take a picture of our newborn daughters laying side-by-side in Suzanne's bassinet.

Spring of 1983: After six years and three babies in Boston, I want to move back to Philadelphia. My parents still live there. So do the other grandparents. And my two sisters and their husbands. Preston says O.K., let's do it. The real estate market in Boston has doubled the price of our house. We can buy an older and larger house in Philadelphia and renovate it for the same price. Good-bye, Birthright. Farewell, Janice and William. Good-bye, Boston.

Philadelphia, PA., Halloween, 1983: Preston has decided to start up his own business in our new parlor-turned-office. We've bought an abandoned Victorian twin next door to my sister and her husband. It is in the residential neighborhood adjacent to the university we all attended. Many of our college and church acquaintances still live here. Like ourselves, most are now married and have young children. These people all knew me when I was unmarried and pregnant.

The pastor who recommended the adoption agency to me, and who later married us, has just bought the house on the other side of us. His wife and I each gave birth to baby boys five months apart. The adorable freckle-faced little boy next door is a constant reminder of my lost son.

1984 and 1985: It feels like a time-released bomb is exploding within my heart. I begin to attend a local support group for birth mothers. I can no longer hide, repress nor deny my loss. It is staring at me, every day, in the eyes of my three little daughters. What if my son has asthma, like Leigh? Is he even alive? Is he happy? He is calling out to me. I know he needs me.

I know I need professional counseling. I am referred to a psychiatrist who specializes in adolescents and adoption issues. Dr. Schechter published several articles in medical journals after noticing how many of his patients were adoptees. His wife is an adoptee. He has long pondered the significance of genetic ties. His Rx: "Mrs. Barton, you need to find your son." He is the first professional to affirm my need. The good doctor's "prescription" gives me the added courage and permission which I need, to proceed with what my heart has long told me I must do. Now, whenever my family or friends tell me that I am crazy to search for such a young child, I can tell them, "My shrink says I would be crazier not to."

1986: I have come full circle to give birth to my last child, like my first, in Philadelphia. I choose to deliver the baby in the privacy of a birthing center, rather than in the maternity ward of a hospital. *Madeleine is my first child to be conceived with the understanding that she will not replace her brother, and that I will love her every bit as much.

1989: It has taken me four years to find my son, and another to finally see him. I had expected to find a slightly malad-justed, but an otherwise "normal" twelve-year-old adopted boy. Jacob has the body, mind and mannerisms of a six-year-old. His dwarfed limbs and high-pitched voice make him seem younger than my Chloe, who is only ten. Instead of missing out on twelve years of his life, it feels like I've only foregone the first six. He resembles me more than any one of my four girls.

1993: An autographed copy of Nancy Verrier's *The Primal Wound* has been sitting on my bookshelf for over a year. I cannot bring myself to read more than a few pages. Did the primal wound of abandoning my baby worsen his disabili-ties? Or are his limitations a blessing in disguise? He will for-ever be a child, forever a minor . . . I may never be able to explain these things to him, or to ask his forgiveness. If he has not been spared the primal wound, maybe he will never be consciously aware of it. Either way, I never want to counsel another unwed or prospective birth mother again. I need to work on my own regrets.

@ *The Leap Year Father* @

Date: Apr. 7 21:37:34 ET
From: ElisaMB@aol.com
To: Mailing list for Birthparents

In my sophomore year of college, I was on the rebound from a broken heart, determined not to fall in love again. I decided to do what I now recognize as a pattern: I fled as far away as I could get from the source of my pain.

I had just begun to study German, loved the language and was considering majoring in it. A study-abroad program fell into my lap, and I grabbed at the chance to fly away. My goal was to forget the American boyfriend who'd dumped me; to enjoy myself without becoming emotionally dependent on another man. At the age of nineteen, I believed that I could separate the physical from the emotional aspects of a relationship.

In the quaint Baroque university town of Bonn, at the student dormitory where I lived, I soon met the perfect person for my purposes. He was seven years older than me. He was kind, funny, intelligent, energetic, and entertaining. I felt invulnerable around him, because I wasn't in love. *Friedrich wooed me relentlessly, literally sweeping me off my feet at the dorm party where we first met, dancing to Joan Baez's rendition of *The Night They Drove Old Dixie Down.*

Early in the morning after the dance party, I was awakened by a soft tapping at my dorm room door. Friedrich stood there with a tray full of salamis, freshly baked Brötchen and an invitation to a private breakfast. Beyond his frantic domesticity, Friedrich was an incurable romantic. He made a great housewife.

Over the next several months, he did everything within his limited power to gain entrance to my heart. My semester study abroad program, however, was drawing to a close. Friedrich was determined to keep me in Germany. I turned down his proposal of marriage, but accepted his assistance in securing a job at a nearby embassy. I extended my leave of absence from college for another semester.

The discrepancy in our feelings for one another became increasingly and painfully apparent. I tried to distance myself from him but found that he had become my closest friend. I was reluctant to give him up entirely, at least not until my return to the United States.

Completing my undergraduate degree was the excuse I gave him when I prepared to leave Germany at the end of a full year's stay. The more I insisted that I was really leaving, the more Friedrich denied it. On the morning that I departed Bonn, Friedrich came to my place as usual, fully expecting to find me there. That image of him, standing there in utter disbelief at my abandonment, haunted me for many years to come.

Back in Philadelphia again, I discovered that I was carrying his child. I, too, had been in a complete state of denial over my pregnancy. Friedrich was joyful upon receiving the news, hopeful that I'd now return to Germany for good, and marry him. I offered to bring him the baby, to raise by himself. Between the two of us, I felt he would make the better single parent. But he did not want the baby without the wife. And I did not want to marry him in order to keep the baby. He was entirely opposed to the idea of adoption. He told me I would be better off having an abortion.

I began pre-adoption counseling instead. From one week, letter, or phone call to the next, I would tell Friedrich to hop on the next overseas flight. Then I would change my mind and tell him to cancel his plans.

After our child was born, I sent him a brief message containing the baby's birth statistics and the few tidbits of information I had been given about the adoptive family. Friedrich's reaction to my decision to place our child for adoption had seemed definite and final. He had written, "The boy is dead to me. Don't ever mention him to me again. I cannot live with the knowledge that a son of mine is out there in the world, and I cannot know him." After receiving his congratulatory response to my wedding announcement, I expected there to be no more communication between us.

Four years later, however, he telephoned me from Germany. His call coincided with the birth of my second daughter, and with the dawning realization that the pain of losing the first child was never going to disappear, no matter how many other children I conceived, bore, raised, and adored. I had begun to have a recurring thematic dream about returning to Germany with the baby in my arms, trying to locate the birth father. In the dream, I kept missing trains, or ending up in the wrong country, or speaking the wrong language, and never quite reaching Bonn or Friedrich.

I said, "Oh, Friedrich, what a coincidence that you called. I've just had this dream . . ." Friedrich never did explain why he was calling. He refused to discuss our son. He listened to what I told him about the baby, about my letter to the adoptive family, about my "Germany dreams," but he remained silent and then changed the subject. He said something about a new girlfriend from the Philippines.

Over the next several years, I made a conscious decision to find our son. I resolved also to keep in touch with the birth father, so that I could at least have an address to pass on to our son. At one point, I had to write to the American Embassy in Bonn, in order to obtain Friedrich's change of address. Coincidence and irony would have it that his wife, the same Philippine he had mentioned on the phone, was working at the American Embassy, and my letter was passed to her. So this is how Friedrich ended up telling his wife about me and our baby. He had to explain the meaning of a letter from "some crazy American woman" who was desperately seeking *her* husband!

When I finally saw our son, I sent Friedrich a photograph which my husband had taken of Jacob, his best friend and myself. The letter was merely the photo, and an invitation to ask questions. The birth father never replied.

Four years later, I was to return to Europe for the first time in sixteen years. I was uncertain about whether I should try to see Friedrich, so I took the open-ended approach again, writing, "I'll be passing through Germany. Let me know if you care to get together." He telephoned right away, inviting me to stay with his family.

I hesitated for the remaining months before the trip. I was a nervous wreck. I had no idea why, except that it had more to do with lost parents rather than with a lost child. I wrote to his wife, seeking her reassurance. Friedrich replied in her place, reiterating that his wife was eager to meet me. My husband could not accompany me, so I asked two dear American friends to join me. Ann flew with me from Philadelphia. Paul was working in Holland, and Ann and I met him at the Bonn train station.

The first day and night under Friedrich's roof were difficult. I saw the same look of pain in his ice-blue eyes which I had shunned sixteen years earlier, as I had flippantly said *auf wiedersehen* and walked out of his life. In addition to the hurt that

I'd personally inflicted, I recognized many of the symptoms of "birthparenthood": overwhelming love and helpless retreat; unjustified fits of anger with his beloved wife and children; guilt; depression; self-deceit and self-defeat. The pain for him had been just as real, but we seemed to have suffered it differently. He had chosen a course of oblivion and denial and was seemingly stuck there. Searching for and finding my son had begun to release me from the deep freeze to some degree. But Friedrich seemed buried frozen, with no concept of any need to thaw out.

I knew that I still had great difficulty forgiving myself for having abandoned our baby. I realized that I needed Friedrich's forgiveness as well.

What was I doing under the roof of this man, his wife, his three children, and their live-in Filipino baby-sitter? By the second evening, I understood that Friedrich was not going to ask me any significant questions. I asked his wife to accompany me on a walk, while the birth father remained warily behind with my friends Paul and Ann.

His wife reminded me so much of myself that it was eerie. But we immediately liked one another. As we walked and talked, she kept saying, "Oh! Now I understand why Friedrich . . ." There had been other relationships where one partner had basically used and discarded the other, but his and mine had eluded any resolution over all these years. The pregnancy, my marriage, and the time and distance between us, had preempted any closure. But healing the wounds of our broken relationship, she said, were necessary for her husband's private sense of peace. She encouraged me to force the issue by openly sharing my feelings with Friedrich; to crack open the shell, even though, she warned, his initial reaction may be ugly.

It happened almost exactly as Friedrich's wife had predicted. I gave him the chance to vent his anger at me, at himself, and at fate. I sincerely apologized for the way I had treated him. He angrily confessed that he had married his wife when she had become pregnant with their oldest child; he had refused to commit that mistake twice. Their marriage had been lopsided for many years, with his wife always feeling beholden to him, and with him feeling penned in. There was still no mention of our son.

The following morning, Friedrich brought out his home movies. Ann, Paul, and I sat with his wife and children watching one birth event or family celebration after another. When Friedrich was shown wearing a yellow hospital gown and holding his third newborn in his arms, I felt the urge to cry, and I left the room.

Friedrich came to look for me and asked what had upset me. I wondered out loud why the birth of his three subsequent children had not triggered the same comprehension and pain for him that these parallel events had for me. He thought about my question and then asked me whether I had nursed any of my babies. I replied that I had breast-fed all four of my daughters, but not our son.

The eggshell began to crack. After sixteen years, we had finally returned to the moment of our son's birth. The questions and answers began to flow. He asked to see more photos of our son. I caught him up with what little I understood about the past, present, and future of our mentally- and physically-handicapped son. He asked me to please give him more time to digest these things.

Friedrich had made a scrapbook of all of our correspondence. Within its pages, he had carefully stored the relinquishment papers which the adoption agency had sent. He showed them to me now, and apologized for never having signed nor returned them. I told him that, if I had needed to lose my son to another family, I wished that it had been to him and to his family.

The following morning was the second Sunday in May. I awoke to find myself with my son's father, in Germany, on a sunny *Muttertag*. My son may never know that I am his mother. My four daughters were an ocean away. The father of my firstborn child gently kissed me and said, "Happy Mother's Day."

Another leap-year has passed since that *Muttertag*, and I will soon be traveling back to Europe. My husband says, "Leave the poor guy alone; he needs a good long rest after your last visit!" The timing seems right, however. It has been four years since our last confession.

@ *Regrets* @

Date: 29 July 18:22:45 EDT
From: ElisaMB@aol.com
To: bmoms@abcd.edu

Lately, I've been asking myself a lot of questions. Why haven't I ever been able to say, like some other birth mothers do, that for this or that reason, adoption was the best choice for my baby and for me? Is it just that I am of a highly opinionated nature, that I prefer to see things as white or black but never gray? Is it because my initial hopes and dreams for my baby's life and for my own subsequent life have been shattered? Why has my sense of loss increased rather than decreased over the years? Am I just a selfish and spoiled ingrate? Why have I never been able to comes to terms with my life sentence to birthmotherhood, or with my son's fate to live his life as an adoptee?

I am highly opinionated and headstrong. I do prefer to see things as either black or white. I tend to ignore the gray areas in between. If I had to give my overall personal philosophy of adoption, it would be similar to my personal religious and political philosophies: I believe in absolutes. I eschew relativism wherever possible. And yes, I'm a spoiled and selfish ingrate.

When it comes to answering the "How" and "Why" questions, however, I am forced to set aside my absolutist tendencies and to review the relative givens and facts surrounding not only the period of time when I was pregnant, but all that has happened to me and to my surrendered child since we parted ways. This is where the rubber finally meets the road. Because what has happened to each of us since our separation indicates to me that my son and I should have remained together from the beginning.

I cannot say, or even pretend, that I was not equipped to become the best mother in the world to my baby. I was not a teenager. I was a few credits away from obtaining a bachelor of arts degree from an Ivy League university. My parents had the resources to help me, and even if they hadn't, I had the wherewithal to help myself. I was not addicted to drugs or to alcohol, to caffeine or to nicotine. When the most prestigious infertility specialist and obstetrician in Philadelphia offered his outstanding obstetrical services to me pro-bono in exchange for surrendering my baby to one of his private infertility patients, I turned him down. I searched out the best maternity hospital in the area, and found a way to finance the hospital bills. I borrowed a friend's car to go for my prenatal visits. I attended birthing classes accompanied by my mother.

Throughout my pregnancy, I researched all of the alternatives I had available. I sought out counselors of every kind, from clergymen to social workers to adoptees, to family and friends. I sought out any birth mother I could find (in 1976, there were not very many willing to admit it) and asked questions about her decision, and about life since relinquishment. I asked everyone for help and advice in making the decision between adoption or single parenting.

I earned my first 4.0 in college that term, due probably to taking naps between classes. I won several academic awards that semester. The baby was due in July, which was perfect as far as the academic calendar was concerned.

As soon as the baby was born, the social worker from the adoption agency came to the hospital with a lawyer. They said that the baby's father had never returned the forms relinquishing his rights but that this presented no great problem. The lawyer simply needed to place a small legal notice in a German newspaper. If the "alleged father" did not come forth to claim his child within two weeks of publication, his paternal rights were forfeited.

The night before I signed the papers, I beseeched my mother to help me keep my son. She told me that I was strong enough to do what was best for the baby, and that my son needed a family with two parents. In the morning, I signed the papers and left the hospital. The social worker said she would be taking the baby to a foster family that same day, and then to his adoptive family. That was the first of many untruths I was later to discover.

Now here are the facts, as they unraveled after I gave up the baby. I left the hospital and went home to my parents' house, where I had not been welcomed since the fifth month of the pregnancy. No one mentioned the baby. My milk came in abundantly, even though I had taken those little red pills. My parents bought me a plane ticket to Miami and to San Juan, and sent me on a little vacation. I cried only late at night, when there was no one around to see or to hear me.

My valiant new boyfriend had spent the summer trying to convince his parents that I was the woman he wanted to marry. My future father-in-law objected more to my non-Anglo-saxon heritage than to the fact that I was a tainted woman. Several months later, I numbly repeated my wedding vows.

My husband knew what he was getting into when he chose this fiery Cuban as his bride, but neither of us had the slightest idea how deeply "birthmotherhood" would affect our marriage. I fell in and out of deep depressions all the time. My husband was always very supportive. If anything, he tended to overdo it, blaming himself for not having married me sooner, so that we could have raised my son together.

And there's the biggest rub: ever since my son's infancy, I have been acutely aware of the fact that my husband could have been my son's adoptive father. Preston would have married me, in fact sooner, had I decided to keep the baby. My son would now have his four little half-sisters. I would not trade my four subsequent daughters for the world, but I also know that, had I never married, I would have made an excellent single mother to my special-needs son.

Instead, this is what my son got: a set of unrelated adoptive parents who are less educated than either myself or my husband. Parents who are financially less advantaged than we are. An adoptive father who appears to have abandoned his wife and their two adoptive children when my son was less than twelve years old. An older adopted sister who is so protective of my son that she writes to me that her multiple-handicapped brother is "fine" and to leave them alone.

As you can see, I have many regrets. They are not just based on fantasies. There is one "what if," however, that I wish to share with you now.

A few months after I'd located my son, but before I had seen him, I was having a conversation with my brother-in-law and next-door-neighbor, *Gary. My older sister and her husband had been trying to conceive their first child for a long time. Gary was trying to make me understand how awful it is to face the possibility of never having a child of one's own. By then, I was quite hardened in my opinion about infertile couples adopting other peoples' babies. My son had probably been adopted by such a couple.

Eventually, our conversation came around to the day I went home from the hospital without the baby. I remembered very little, but Gary had been at my parents' house that day, and he remembered everything. Right after my mother and I had walked in the front door, my father had led Gary into the kitchen and whispered: "Where's the baby?"

In the ten years which had passed since that day, no one had ever mentioned this. Had my father asked me that question, or had my brother-in-law told me at the time, I would have immediately hailed a taxi back to the hospital to reclaim my son; to hell with the papers I had just signed!

I sometimes struggle over whom, or what, I need most to "forgive and forget": myself, my father, my brother-in-law, or my God?

@ *"Return to Sender"* @

Date: Nov. 14 2:42 PM EST
From: ElisaMB@aol.com
To: Adoption Triad Mailing List

Dear Internet Friends:

My son Jacob has four younger half-sisters. They each share half of the same genetic pool as Jacob. They look like him. They have each been told about him as they have grown old enough to understand. Because we are a family of all girls and no boys, the fact of their older half-brother has come up repeatedly and in a natural way. I chose never to lie to them or to others, when the question of a brother or of a son was raised in a genuine manner.

I have spoken to Jacob's adoptive mother once, when Jacob was twelve years old. In that telephone conversation, she told me that since Jacob had not yet begun to ask questions about how babies come into the world, she had not told him that he had been born to another mother. I assumed that she would explain his adoption to him eventually, at a time and in a manner which was appropriate to his level of understanding.

Years passed, and she never replied to any of my letters. The pastor of their church offered to speak to her on my behalf. He related parts of that conversation. Jacob, then sixteen, still had not been told anything about us because it would only "upset and confuse him."

Do you adoptees think that Jacob might be capable of understanding what adoption means to him if his sister or his mother were to say something like, "Jacob, it means that you have another mother and four younger sisters who care about you and who would someday like to meet you."?

I have beheld my son twice in my entire life. I gave birth to him without the help of any anesthetic drugs. My mother attended childbirth classes with me and was with me throughout the labor and the delivery. There were two Scottish nurse-midwives and one obstetrician in the delivery room. The newborn baby was placed directly on top of my chest as I lay on the delivery room table. I had removed my contact lenses and was wearing my glasses. The first thing my son did was to pee directly into my eyeglasses. I counted his perfectly formed ten fingers and ten toes. I gazed into a face which looked so much like my own that it astounded me. His hair, his eyes, his nose, and his mouth were identical to my own.

Over the next several days in the hospital, he was brought to me and I was permitted to visit him in the baby nursery, once or twice. I fed him, held him, rocked him, sang and cried to him, changed his diapers and bathed him. On the second day, I was told that he was having problems keeping down the baby formula. I had been advised not to breast-feed him because it might make me too attached to him and would thus make it harder to say good-bye. But I wanted him to have my antibodies. One kind nurse told me that I could express my colostrum into a baby bottle and then feed it to him. He immediately gulped down my natural milk and digested it without any problem. Several family members and friends came to visit me and to leave gifts for the baby. I recall a little blue elephant, a bunny, and a blue baby outfit, all of which I gave to the adoption agency social worker to pass on to his adoptive parents.

Many years later, when I finally got up the nerve to request our hospital records, I found out that Jacob had not left the hospital on the same day that I had been discharged. The social worker from the adoption agency had promised me that she would be taking my son from the hospital with her that day, to put him in the care of one of their foster families.

After a month of "observation," my baby would then go to his permanent adoptive home. But after I had signed the relinquishment papers and left the hospital myself, my baby was transferred into the intensive care unit. He was still vomiting the formula. The newborn records show that he was not discharged for another week. I was never informed because, by then, I was no longer his legal guardian.

The fact that my newborn baby was left all alone in that hospital nursery, for an entire week, greatly troubles me to this day. The agency social worker lived in another state, almost a three-hour drive from the hospital. I was all of five minutes away from my baby, and never knew it.

I had never been told, by the doctors or by the adoption agency, that my baby was anything but healthy and normal. At birth he had an almost perfect APGAR score of nine. Jacob now has a total of seven half-siblings, none of whom have any mental or physical disabilities. When I was told that Jacob was registered at the Special Olympics, I feared and imagined every conceivable explanation for what may have befallen him since his birth. My husband and I decided to drive up to this public event to see Jacob.

The Parade of Athletes started up and I noticed a boy in a bright blue jacket. He was shorter and more overweight than I had imagined him, but I immediately knew that this was the infant I had once held in my arms. I fell into step behind him and stood next to him throughout the Opening Ceremonies. He was holding a tongue depressor in his hand. The boy turned to me, smiled, and said, "Lollipop!" He showed me his name in the list of athletes.

The Games began and continued throughout the day. We watched Jacob run in circles inside a gymnasium. He'd finally shed his long-sleeved jacket and for the first time I noticed his dwarfed arms, the shortness of his breath and the rosiness of his cheeks whenever he exerted an unusual amount of energy. (Two of our daughters are asthmatics and react similarly when they over-exert themselves.) Jacob then moved outdoors and won first place in the 50-meter race! We stood far back and watched him proudly receive his gold medal on the podium. We watched him shoot basketballs and receive prizes of Hawaiian necklaces and other such trinkets. We saw him in the ball toss and heard his sister and mother both yell at him simultaneously, "Use your left hand, Jake!" Prior to this, I had not realized that my son was left-handed. Another oddity, as every one of his birth relatives is right-handed.

During the five-hour drive home, I saw my husband cry for the first time. He had known that my son existed all along, he had even felt the baby kicking me while I was pregnant. But in all our years of marriage, the reality of my son's separate life had never hit him in quite the same way. We discussed the future medical and psychological implications for Jacob, as well as the possible medical ramifications for our daughters. We decided that, upon our return to Philadelphia, it would be best to consult with a genetic specialist. We were also concerned about the absence of Jacob's adoptive father.

I have lost several precious things which I can never hope to replace or to regain. I have lost my firstborn child. I have lost a great deal of trust in basic human decency, especially with regard to the system of adoption as it is practiced in this country. I have forfeited years of what may have otherwise been a relatively happy marriage and motherhood. I fully realize that my son can never be "Returned to Sender," like an unopened letter. But what more do I really stand to lose, by seeking to reunite with my son? I only stand to regain certain things . . . such as a sense of peace and security about his future. Perhaps a feeling of mutual trust with his adoptive family. Perhaps a greater sense of self-respect.

No woman ever becomes a mother, gives her child away, and then just goes on with her life as if it never happened.

Can a mother forget her infant? Be without love for the fruit of her womb? Even should she forget, I would not forget. (Isaiah 49:15).

That was God speaking. Neither God nor I have ever forgotten Jacob. Neither of us ever will.

CHAPTER TWO

Stairway to Heaven

*Lyrics by Jimmy Page and Robert Plant
of Led Zeppelin, 1971*

There's a lady who's sure all that
glitters is gold. And she's buying a staircase to heaven.
And when she gets there she knows
if the stores are closed
with a word she can get what she came for.

There's a sign on the wall
but she wants to be sure
'Cause you know sometimes words have
two meanings.
In a tree by the brook there's a songbird
who sings. Sometimes
all of our thoughts are misgiven.

There's a feeling I get when I look
to the west
and my spirit is crying for leaving.
In my thoughts I have seen rings of smoke
through the trees
and the voices of those who stand looking.

And it's whispered that soon if we all
call the tune
then the piper will lead us to reason.
And a new day will dawn for those
who stand long.
And the forests will echo with laughter.
And it makes me wonder.
If there's a bustle in your hedgerow
Don't be alarmed now.
It's just a spring clean for the May-Queen.
Yes there are two paths you can go by
but in the long run
there's still time to change the road you're on.

Your head is humming and it won't go
—in case you don't know.
The piper's calling you to join him.
Dear lady can you hear the wind blow?
And did you know
Your stairway lies on the whispering wind?

And as we wind on down the road
our shadows taller than our soul
there walks a lady we all know
who shines white light and wants to show
how everything still turns to gold.
And if you listen very hard
The tune will come to you at last
When all are one and one is all
To be a rock and not to roll.

@ *Pounded in the Fire* @

Date: July 30 07:58:23 EDT
From: Gateway@aol.com
To: ElisaMB@aol.com

Elisa, it sounds like the last twenty years of your life have been about deep regret and loss. You've really struggled with this and can see no good in it. Sometimes, when I'm in that place, I find it useful to ask myself: What has this experience taught me about life and about myself? How has it changed what is important to me?

Life has many ways of preparing us. When a blacksmith wants to forge a rod of iron into a beautiful object, he sticks it in the fire and pounds the hell out of it.

I've felt myself in that fire being pounded, too. It hurts! But if one can come to understand the purpose of the artist, one can come to marvel at the process and the end it achieves.

Love and blessings, Gateway

@ *That Little Bracelet* @

Date: Feb. 24 1:00 PM EDT
From: Kate@Dartmouth.edu
To: ElisaMB@aol.com

These discussions of holding our babies has brought up a memory long buried. I must say I treasure bringing it back to consciousness.

I was one of those mothers who was not allowed to hold my baby. My mother and I just looked through the glass of the nursery window. The baby was lying there looking around, but moments after our arrival, she started to cry. I made a joke about how she was trying to make me feel guilty. (How disassociated I was from my feelings!) I asked the nurses if I could hold my baby and they said no. Finally a nurse picked her up and held her up in front of the glass. I wanted to tell the nurse to comfort her, but said nothing. It seemed to me she was being held like a loaf of bread rather than as a baby.

I remember seeing that little bracelet on the baby's wrist. Later I asked the nurse (and this is the unburied memory) rather sheepishly, "What do you do with those little bracelets when the babies go home?" She could see where I was going with my question and said, "Now, dear. You wouldn't want to keep a reminder of something you need to put behind you . . ." or some such words of wisdom.

I wanted that little bracelet so much, but was made to feel foolish for even asking. I wanted it so I could hold it . . . take it out of its hiding place every once in a while and just look at it . . . an "Identification Bracelet." It carried more power and importance to those people in the hospital than I did. It was official. It identified the baby as my daughter to the world, if only for a short time. It was one of the few official things that identified her with her true birth information rather than with her "amended" information. I wish I had it now to present to my daughter when I find her: a memento of her connection to her birth mother.

Being denied that little bracelet! It is this kind of experience that contributes to our beliefs that we don't count, that our feelings are wrong or inappropriate, and that other people know better what is good for us and what is not. Our psyches never forget. These memories accumulate. Through compounded interest, we end up with "post-traumatic stress disorder," low self-esteem, addiction problems, relationship problems, generalized depression, victim-consciousness . . . the list goes on.

Truth, and the loving support of others come along, and against phenomenal odds, we begin, and we continue, the process of healing.

Kate

@ *Finding Anna* @

Date: June 11 8:44:22 AM EDT
To: DJ@aol.com
From: ElisaMB@aol.com

Lieber Deroll Johan: Get used to responding to that name again. I have a strong feeling you are embarking on a return journey to a place where you will begin to heal, to reconcile your two selves, to integrate your past and present lives into a new and promising future. Here's how to get ready:

1) Call the overseas operator or international directory assistance. You simply dial 011 or 00 on your phone at home. This will connect you with a U.S. international operator. You tell him or her you're looking for Anna Maierschoffer and give them her last known address in Germany. Don't tell them it is from 1959. Make sure you get the spelling absolutely right. Read it straight from the original documents you have.

The U.S. operator will stay on the line with you and you'll hear her calling the German one, probably in Munich since that's the closest major city to Augsburg. Then the American operator will repeat all the information to the German one, who will look up what they have on the books in Germany. All you have to do is sit there and listen. The German operator will speak to the American one in English. If you spoke German you could interrupt the conversation between the operators and speak to the German one directly, and the U.S. operator wouldn't understand anything but would continue to facilitate the communication.

International directory assistance used to be free of charge, but now it costs a few dollars. Make sure the operators check all the Maierschoffers in Augsburg, first on the particular street name you had from 1959, and at the Bocksberg address. If there are no Maierschoffers listed at either address, ask them to give you the name, address and telephone for any Maier-schoffer in either or both towns. You don't need to go into any explanations, but if directory assistance begins to grow weary or suspicious, say something like, "It's my long-lost sister! We are both orphans and were separated a long time ago and I have to find her!!!" That should pull the right heartstrings with both operators and they will probably bend over backwards, looking up every living Maierschoffer in all of Germany.

I would pick up the phone and do all of this for you in a minute except that it is important for you to do as much of it by and for yourself as possible. With every step you take to control your own future, you will begin to regain the control which was taken from you in the past.

2) Start relearning German as quickly as you can! You'll be surprised at how much you will remember; at how relatively effortlessly you will understand it, and will begin to speak it again. The first five years of your *Muttersprache* is not gone, DJ; it is merely lying dormant, underneath several layers of time and trauma. It can all be recaptured without undergoing hypnosis. Buy yourself some Berlitz tapes or a self-tutoring computer program and get started. As soon as you are ready, we can switch into German on-line so you can practice fur-ther (except that there are no umlauts on e-mail).

3) Set aside at least a week of vacation time for yourself and buy yourself a round-trip ticket to either Stuttgart or Munich. (Augsburg is in between the two. I can't find Bocksberg on my maps of Germany. I'm sure it's a minuscule village, but I'd guess it's not far from Augsburg.) If you are not able to locate your mother from here, you should still plan a trip to Ger-many. You're certain to find many remnants of your former

life there; what's become of the orphanage and its other inhabitants and workers; perhaps other living relatives. If you'd like, when the time comes, I could meet you in Germany and serve as an interpreter. I'm fairly familiar with the region around Stuttgart and have good friends and contacts.

Aufwiederlesen und alles Gute, Elisa

@ *RE: Finding Anna* @

Date: June 11 18:44:26 EDT
From: DJ@aol.com
To: ElisaMB@aol.com

Dear Elisa,

All my life I have felt like I had two separate existences. De-roll Maierschoffer, the German Child, and Michael Parker, the American boy. The duplicity in my life has been difficult to reconcile, and I don't think I ever will, until I see my mother and father, either in the flesh, or in a photograph.

To fill you in on some of my history, I remember many of my "siblings" in the orphanage. We ate communally and bathed in groups. There was a tribal atmosphere about the place. There was a woman there who had eyes like Jesus, sweet, kind eyes that made me feel safe whenever I looked into them. There was another woman who had eyes like cold steel. I was always afraid of her somewhat, but I knew that if anyone bothered me, she would turn those eyes on them and they would leave me alone. She, too, made me feel safe in her own way.

My adoption was the most terrifying experience of my entire life. We went out on the front porch of the orphanage, and some pictures were taken. The next thing I knew, these two strangers, with whom I could not communicate, were hus-tling me off to a car. (I spoke no English, and my father and mother spoke no German.) When we reached the car, I balked. I remember fighting my father like a wild animal. I thought they were taking me to be killed. When they got me in the car, my mother drove, and my father handed me a teddy bear. I threw the teddy bear out of the car window as soon as he handed it to me. I then promptly attempted to jump from the car. I managed to get my entire upper body out of the car window. My father clamped tight around my waist and legs and dragged me back into the car. I remember kicking, screaming, biting . . . a pretty nasty scene. In the end, he (230 lb., 6' 4") physically held me down in the car seat. When we reached "home," they locked me into a room to stop any further escape attempts. I felt like a trapped animal.

We left Germany a few days later. As we were aboard the ship, I remember looking out over the waves and thinking that I had never felt so alone. I remember being very sad. I could not have felt more alienated. I remember thinking that I would never again see all the people that I had come to love as brothers and sisters in my short little life. In the space of one day, I lost every person that was ever dear to me. I lost my language, my culture, my surroundings. I remember feeling as though I had been carried off to another planet. The children I had played with in the orphanage were like my brothers and sisters. The children that I met in America were taunting strangers. I remember being called "Nazi" by the other Catholic school children. At the time, I didn't even know what the term meant. To put it mildly, it was a nightmarish experience.

According to the papers, I was born "out of wedlock." Having figured my birth date against that of my mother, she was twenty-two at the time. She is listed as "domestic help," which I assume to have been a maid. There is no record of who my father is.

My father has told me that my birth mother contacted him at one point and asked that I be returned to her. But he told her that he felt that I had been "bounced back and forth" enough and declined to return me, stating that I needed stability in my life. I was unaware of this until I became an adult.

I got the documents out of my parents' file box in their bedroom, some twenty years ago. I needed a copy of my adoption decree, my original birth certificate, and my naturalization papers, to join the U.S. Army. The only thing I have which connects me directly to my birth mother is the signature of Anna Maierschoffer on my birth certificate.

I have never been back to Germany since I was adopted. I've always wanted to return, but the time has never seemed right. One thing that has always puzzled me is why I have blocked out the German language. I guess I should attempt to relearn it at some point. Maybe it's the old fear of the unknown. I worry that if I were to begin speaking German again, all those terrifying feelings might come flooding back.

Well, I've got to get ready for work. Thanks again. I'll give the overseas operator a try and see what kind of luck I have. Deroll Johan Maierschoffer, also known as Michael Parker.

@ *Orphan Voyages* @

Date: June 11 20:34 EDT
To: DJ@aol.com
From: ElisaMB@aol.com

Dear Michael:

It was painful for me to read your adoption story because I have shared similar experiences. You were born in Augsburg, West Germany in 1955 to a German mother. In 1960 you were brought to this country by American adoptive parents. As five-year-olds, you and I both had to suddenly adapt ourselves to a new culture, a new family, and a new language. Although neither of us were true orphans, we experienced what many adoptees know as the "orphan voyage."

I was born in 1955 as well, but in Havana, Cuba. In 1958, my parents were imprisoned for helping to send ammunition to Castro's men. We spent a year in exile in the U.S. fleeing Batista's regime. When Castro won the revolution, we returned to Cuba. My father was appointed to Fidel's first cabinet. Within a year and a half of the new regime, we had to flee a second time. We escaped on the final ferry boat between Havana Harbor and the Florida Keys. We came to Philadelphia because the Cuban-American branch of the family had resided here for several generations.

In the months which followed my parents' incarceration, and then again briefly in 1960, my older sister and I were separated from our parents and from our younger siblings. Like yourself, we were too young to understand whether or when we would see our family again.

Assimilating into a new culture was as difficult as you described it. I experienced the same problems with the new language and in the Catholic schools. The children were sometimes as cruel to me as the nuns were to all of us, taunting me for my lack of comprehension, or because my ears were pierced. I was embarrassed to invite kids over to my house because my parents spoke Spanish.

In high school, I spent a year in an Alpine French village, as an exchange student. I lived with two diametrically opposed French families, learning a third language and culture from scratch. I was unprepared for the resurgent sadness of the difficult adjustments I'd made as a young Cuban refugee. It was difficult trying to reconcile the two identities about which you spoke: the fully-Americanized and self-confident teenager, with the timid exchange student who spoke and felt like a pre-schooler in this quaint French town and at its lycee.

During college my life began all over again in Germany. But that's another long story, for another time.

@ *Post-Traumatic Adoption Syndrome* @

Date: July 13 18:39 EST
From: ElisaMB@aol.com
To: DJ@aol.com

My dear Deroll Johan Michael Anthony Maierschoffer Parker!
One of these days you're going to read it in a book, or recognize it in another adoptee's words, and a light-bulb will go off
in your own head, that you are suffering from "post-traumatic adoption syndrome."

We birth parents have it too, you know, only it is manifested
a bit differently. The symptoms for most adoptees are: an
overwhelming sense of anger, which, for reasons inexplicable
even to themselves, end up coming out as the opposite. They
are overly and unnecessarily apologetic; they often feel and
act beholden or grateful to others for the simplest acts of human kindness; they have an irrational fear of desertion by
those who truly care for them.

Think about it, Michael; read over your letters to me, a virtual
stranger to you. Why do you keep apologizing to me? Why
do you keep expressing this fear that you are overburdening me or that you've offended me in some way? You are
incapable of offending me! It was I who decided to reply to
the message you publicly posted on America Online. It was
I who thrust myself into your business, not the other way
around!

If I sound angry, Michael, I am. But not at you! I'm angry at a
system of adoption which cripples otherwise innocent, sweet,
intelligent and kind children and turns them into wounded
adults who are so bewildered by it all, they don't know how
to begin to heal. I am angry because I recognize some of the
same symptoms in myself, and I don't know how to deal with

them any better. I become angry and fearful when I think about my own dear son; when I imagine any harm which my abandonment may have inflicted upon him.

Perhaps someone in the military will recognize the name of Anna's husband. I'm putting the "Army News" clipping in the regular mail to you today so that you can look over the other ads and compose your own. Send your ad to: Locator File, Army Times, Springfield, VA 22159–0160. Their tel.: (703) 750–8622. My army lawyer friend suggests that you include your name, complete address and phone number.

I am poised ever ready to help you find your lost mother, DJ, be that by translating a letter or a fax into German, or by hopping on the next airplane to Germany.

Aufwiederlesen, Elisa

@ *E.R.* @

Date: Aug. 28 09:28:31 EDT
From: DJ@aol.com
To: ElisaMB@aol.com

Dear Elisa, I just got in from a shift from the hospital. We had a really tough night of it. A car flipped over with two brothers in it. The driver was ejected from the vehicle. He had massive internal injuries, facial fractures, and was very drunk. We flew him out by helicopter to a thoracic surgeon. His brother came into the emergency room in a "Trauma Code." He was in PEA (Pulseless Electrical Activity) when he arrived, with atonal respiration. We put in a chest tube and did the "Code Blue" on him, but we couldn't get his volume up to pull him out of shock. He died a few minutes later. Sometimes my job really shows me the ugly side of life.

I haven't spent much time pushing towards finding Anna. In fact, as I look over the last month or so, I may actually be avoiding it. I would like to find her (I don't want you to feel that I've manipulated you in a self-serving manner) but the fact is that I'm a little afraid of actually finding her, now that all the resources are at my disposal to do so. I guess maybe it's that old fear of the unknown. Each time I think about it, I wonder: Will she want to see me? Will I be emotionally better off with my questions answered? Who is she? Who am I? And I guess I'm afraid that I either won't get the answers that I would like, or, worse yet, to find out that I'm the product of incest or rape, or some other nightmarish event.

I guess I need to sit down and go over my reasons for finding her, and make sure that it is what I want to do before it actually happens. I don't want to intrude on her life, but neither do I want to spend the rest of mine wondering about my origins and about any other family I may have.

I hope this note finds you well and happy. I enjoy reading mail from you and from the others, such as *Magda in Germany, who have so graciously offered to assist. Please forward my thanks to them. I need to rest for tonight (another twelve hours at the E.R.) I'll sign off for now. Be happy, be well, and may God bless and keep you always.

Heartfelt thanks, DJ

@ *Unconditional Love* @

Date: Sept. 8 3:48 AM EST
From: Magda@Uni.Germany
To: ElisaMB@aol.com

Hi, Elisa. Recently there was e-mail from DJ saying that now that he is so close to finding his Mom, he has postponed it, fearing she might not want to see him or that he might be a product of rape, incest, etc.

His mother could die before seeing him. The probability of her wanting to see him, even if he was the product of rape or something similar, is very high. As in my case, when it comes to loving my children, I don't look at what their fathers did to me or to them. I DO hope DJ has found the courage to proceed.

Magda

@ *The Empty Limbs of the Family Tree* @

Date: Jan. 31 3:17 PM EDT
From: ElisaMB@aol.com
To: Adoption Triad Mailing List

As a birth parent, whenever I hear an adoptee describe himself or herself as a "nobody," it makes me both sad and mad. For, if the adoptee is a non-entity, then what does that make me? You may not have been the product of an immaculate conception, but your conception, gestation, and birth are every bit as real to us as your child's is to you!

One of the most insidious aspects of our system of adoption is that it seeks to deny and obliterate the original ties that bind the child and its mother. The brainwashing often begins in the form of prenatal counseling. While you were still inside your mother, already the seeds of disassociation between the two of you had been sown. By the time your mother gave you away to total strangers, she no longer felt she had the right to call herself your mother, or to consider you her own beloved offspring. This is the way it usually works, because it is so rampantly against the instinctive nature of human love and parenthood to explain relinquishment any other way.

When your second-grader goes to draw that family tree for his school project, perhaps you could just add those empty branches for now. Tell your son that some day soon, he'll be able to fill them in with real names and real faces and real blood of his blood and flesh of his flesh. Those empty limbs will surely sprout. They were never dead; they have always existed; they are a part of you and of all of your descendants.

@ *"Birthmother's Choice"* @

Date: Sept. 17 19:24 EST
From: ElisaMB@aol.com
To: Adoption Triad Mailing List

I have to agree with Magda in Germany that «if one is forced to choose between a partner and a child, one should choose the child. Not least because the child needs you the most.»

The question of need is an important one. In the eighteen years since becoming a birth mother, the most painful and heartbreaking realizations have been over the issue of need.

Was it *Saul, the birth father and Hollywood film producer, who made reference to the film *Sophie's Choice*? That story shook me to the depths of my soul as no other Holocaust story ever has. I am certain that it has a lot to do with the choice I made when I became a birth mother. Sophie's was a choice between sending her daughter to a certain death, but of possibly preserving the life of her son; or of dooming both children to the gas chambers. What kind of choice was that? One doesn't need to know Sophie's decision to predict the inevitable consequences. Any mother who is forced to choose between her own life and that of her child, or between the lives of two of her children, is forced to condemn her own soul!

The choice to preserve the unplanned life of my baby was easy compared to all the choices which followed. After my son was born, it came down to a question of need: What are my child's real needs? Who or what will best meet those needs? Once in a while I tried to consider my own needs. Feelings of guilt, shame, and selfishness caused me to repress such considerations.

And yet here is what I have learned about the needs of each of my children: My breast-milk was uniquely designed for them. They knew the rhythm of my heart, the sound of my voice, the smell of my body inside and out, from the moment they emerged from my womb. Their personalities and physical characteristics have always been natural and familiar to me, as mine have always been to them. We spoke the same language before they were born. In short, I was their mother, and they needed me.

I do not see adoption as a question of nurture vs. nature. It is a matter of nature vs. nature. Self-sacrifice for our children may be in our God-given human nature. Giving them away is an aberration of that same nature.

In a life-and-death situation, any loving mother will sacrifice her own needs for those of her child. The true wisdom of King Solomon was his foreknowledge that the infant's true mother would be the woman who would do whatever it took to spare her baby's life, even if it meant giving her child to another woman. The quintessential biblical adoption story, that of Moses, his natural mother, and Pharaoh's daughter, tells the same tale.

Loving, caring, giving and receiving are mutual and reciprocal human needs. I have learned that I need each of my children as much as each of my children needs me.

@ *Head vs. Heart* @

Date: Sept. 17 1:19 AM EST
From: *Celeste@eeyore.edu
To: ElisaMB@aol.com

Elisa, I've shared a couple of your posts with my husband recently and I want you to know that you brought him to tears. I think it helps him immensely to hear how other birth-moms feel, and to understand that I am not alone in my grief. He was not the birth father but has been wonderfully supportive of me in my experience. It's been quite a load for him to bear, that abject agony of someone you love, and your posts have given strength to the both of us.

I can join with you on some levels. We are soul-mates. On others, you are far more adventurous and I cannot follow you to the levels that you explore. I wish sometimes that I could.

The decision to place a child for adoption is a head vs. heart decision. My head always leads but my heart will not, cannot, always comply. My head tells me that I cannot change the circumstances under which I chose adoption for my son— no matter how much my heart wishes it were so. For those of us on this 'Net who lead with the head, there is a new song permeating the airwaves. It both reassures my head and breaks my heart every time I hear it.

Try not to think about what might have been. That was then, and we have taken different roads. We can't go back again. There's no use givin' in. And there's no way to know. . . . What might have been. Keep on keepin' on, Elisa.

Celeste

@ *The Timebomb Theory* @
by Elisa M. Barton

In 1990, the C.U.B. *Communicator* carried an article titled "I Am Glad I Searched For My Minor Son." I wrote: ". . . I have come to believe that most birth parents are living with a time-bomb of pain. It goes off at different times with different people . . . My own timebomb went off about five years ago, when my son was eight years old . . ."

The timebomb symbolizes the encapsulated entirety of a birth mother's pain and grief. I believe that this timebomb is set the minute that she signs the relinquishment papers. But the timer on the bomb is set differently for each birth mother. How, when, and why the bomb detonates is dictated by each birth mother's unique and individual process of grieving, each with its different phases of denial, bargaining, acceptance, and eventual resolution.

A birth mother's ability to realistically respond to that pain is the timebomb which is waiting to go off. It follows some birth mothers into their graves, while exploding in other women's lives while the relinquished child is yet quite young.

I have observed that the timebomb often goes off as soon as the birth mother passes from the denial into the acceptance phase of her grieving; when she comes to the full realization of what happened when she signed those relinquishment papers.

With their permission, I would like to include some of the reactions from a few of the birth mothers on the Internet.

Sara wrote: "As a birth mother involved in a closed adoption in 1964, your theory applies to my life. Thanks for spelling it out. My time bomb exploded about six years ago, but I struggle to this day with searching. I still hang back from giving it my full effort. I get so frightened. I have received many different thoughts from others about whether I even have the right to search."

*Larina, the birth mother of a two-year-old daughter in an open adoption, wrote: "I really didn't care for the whole time bomb analogy, but I did agree that if I had lived in Sweden, I would have gotten to parent my daughter . . ."

Brenda does not believe that the timebomb theory applies to mothers in open adoptions. She explains: "The right to parent: that is what I grieve. Because we see our children as they are growing, we are made aware of the fact of our loss. Yes, there are struggles. Sometimes there is denial of certain feelings. But the openness encourages birth mothers to face those struggles and to overcome them. It allows birth mothers to fully grieve their loss and to come to accept it."

Open vs. Closed Adoptions

When I first considered the timebomb analogy, I was applying it foremost to myself and to the vast majority of birth mothers I had met up until that time. None of them were involved in an open adoption. On the other hand, they had each expressed the sensation of a bomb going off in their lives after many years of repressed grief. The realization of having relinquished our children is very different for those of us who needed and sought, for whatever reason, to deny that reality. The greater and longer the denial or repression, the bigger the explosion!

Birth mothers of children in open adoptions are very much the pioneers of open adoption motherhood in this country. I certainly hope that open adoptions will have a gentler effect on the mothers as well as on the children. If the timebomb theory does not apply to birth mothers in an open adoption, then that is one member of the adoption triad who will be better off. When mothers of minors search for their lost children, it is often with the hope of opening up a previously closed adoption. If we did not believe that this would improve matters for everyone concerned, why would we search?

To make a just comparison between the feelings of a mother who has chosen an open adoption, and those of a mother who was never given the choice, we need to wait until both birth mothers are on an equal plane of information; until the closed adoption has been opened to the same degree. Even once we have searched for, found, and made contact with our lost children, the road from the relinquishment has been so ugly and so painful, that words and feelings such as hope or joy have often been replaced by disillusionment, regret, or rage.

When the Bomb Explodes

For many a birth parent, the detonated timebomb is also the moment in which a decision to search is made. Much the same could be applied to adoptees who decide to search for their birth parents. Whether you are the parent or the adoptee whose timebomb has exploded, the main obstacle to a reunion is an unwritten law which arbitrarily sentences any triad individual to a waiting period of eighteen years. I am reminded of the years during the Vietnam War. How cruel and ridiculous it was to send a nineteen-year-old man to his possible death, in a war decreed by a government for which that same teenager was denied the right to vote!

Birth fathers' motives and reputations, not unlike those of birth mothers, have always been the object of much second-guessing. Some are well-deserved, others quite the opposite. Birth fathers have the added difficulty that they are not necessarily forced to come out of the closet, the way that most birth mothers must, even after many years of repressed guilt or sadness. When a birth father does begin to emerge, he not only has to deal with all of his own baggage, but now also with that of the mother of his surrendered child.

The pain of relinquishment in adoption can only be suppressed for so long. It eventually surfaces and explodes like a timebomb. The bomb victim must figure out what to do with the shrapnel, the wounds, and all the mess. Either the wounds are left untreated and open to infection, or one begins to treat them, and to give them the chance to heal.

Search, Contact, & Reunion: Three Separate Issues

The decision to search is often the best way for adoption triad members to begin to heal the wounds. In particular, a mother chooses to search for her child when and only when she believes she is best able to withstand the inherent and inevitable difficulties involved. Rarely will a searching birth parent jeopardize an eventual or prospective happy reunion by committing an irrevocably stupid act either during the search or throughout the remainder of the adoptee's minority. On the contrary, every birth parent whom I personally know to have searched for and found their minor child, has taken even greater precautions to pave the road for the best possible of future relationships with their child. Most searching adoptees are every bit as considerate in their approach to contact and reunion.

*Scarlett writes: "I surrendered a son born in 1968 and have never tried to search for a number of reasons. I used to believe that the best thing was not to disrupt my son's life, especially since I have no idea if he was even told he was adopted. I was so afraid of reopening this painful part of my life, that I have repressed thoughts of it as much as possible. Like Scarlett O'Hara who put things off to 'think about tomorrow.' I have been afraid of suffering more pain by being rejected. But I have finally decided that I need to begin my search, whatever the consequences, for my own peace of mind. Whether he wants me in his life or not, I need to know if my son is well and happy."

Remember the social workers' line that "you will forget all of this and get on with the rest of your life"? The first part we all know was a myth, but the second part is true for the birth parent who has searched and found. Ask any relative of an MIA what their life was like before they knew for certain whether the missing loved one was dead or alive. The mother or father who knows the name and whereabouts of his or her surrendered child, dead or alive, has a better chance of "getting on with life" than the one who does not.

From the moment the timebomb explodes, we can switch to a different set of analogies. If the mother decides to begin her search at this point, the apt analogies are those of conception (the decision to search); gestation (the process of searching) and finally that of a second birth (finding her lost child.)

Handicapped Survivors

Even for birth parents who are experiencing a happy reunion, the detonated bomb analogy still applies. We, like our rediscovered children, will always have the scars, even after the wounds have healed. We may feel and act like amputees. Our husbands and our subsequent children have been through the same war with us. They have not only witnessed our pain, but also, out of their love and concern for us, have equally had to adapt to our open wounds, our scars, and our lost limbs.

So where do we go from here? Perhaps we birth parents should begin to look around ourselves at real handicapped survivors, to learn from them, and from those who love them as dearly as we are loved. I have had such an opportunity over the last few years.

Luís Winter, a Chilean ambassador, escaped with his life but lost both of his limbs when his government car accidentally tripped a land mine on the border between Chile and Peru. Each of his legs had to be amputated just above the knees. Luís came to Philadelphia for a year of specialized rehabilitation, accompanied by his wife and children. Our children were attending the same school, and I was asked to interpret during a parent-teacher conference. Our families soon became good friends.

Throughout his year at Moss Rehabilitation Hospital, Luís had the prostheses for his legs changed and refitted numerous times. Luís became the first double-amputee in the world to learn to play tennis again! He resumed his daily morning jogs around the neighborhood! He had "waterlimbs" specially made so that he could shower and swim again! He learned to drive a manually-operated vehicle. He struggled daily with acute pain, with infected open sores and wounds, with a grueling schedule of physical and occupational therapy. He had to make constant psychological readjustments, which he admitted were more difficult than the physical ones. His wife and children struggled right alongside him.

Luís asked me to translate his journal into English. Reading about his most intimate struggles taught me much about enduring physical and psychic pain; about replacing fear, anger and desperation with faith and knowledge, with love and hope.

Luís' determination to build a new life for himself was a great inspiration to me. I never told him or his wife that it sometimes feels as if I've lost a limb; I had not given much thought to any such parallels. But when they return to Philadelphia for Luís' yearly consultation, I shall be looking to them anew, for the strength and inspiration to "carry on with my life."

@ *Find Your Daughter* @

Date: Sept. 12 02:48 PM
To: *Rachel@aol.com
From: ElisaMB@aol.com

Dearest Rachel: Some hard heart-to-heart stuff. I am going to save you hours of psychotherapy and marriage counseling and grief over letters from searching mothers or visits or phone calls or their kids' artwork, by simply telling you what you need to do as soon as possible: Find your daughter.

Count yourself lucky that you don't have any other kids yet. At least you don't have to feel guilty about taking anything away from them in terms of your time, dollars, and energy. Sell the dog, sell the car, borrow money for a new roof, do whatever you must in order to FIND YOUR DAUGHTER!

You keep trying to run away from the pain of not knowing by everything you do: forsaking a wonderful employment opportunity in the city where you relinquished your daughter; accepting a low-paying job in a shopping mall half-a-continent away; compiling articles and letters about the very thing which haunts you nightly; worrying over the missing or lost children of other mothers; allowing other mother-and-child reunions or open adoptions to upset you. How could they not? These things will not become any less painful to you until you know where your young daughter is, what her name is, where she lives, how she has fared apart from you since her birth, whether she is even alive!

You are at that moment in your life where you not only can but must proceed in that direction before you do anything else. If you don't, Rachel, you are going to fall deeper into that abyss of depression. The longer you wait to search for her, the harder it will get just to find her. If my "timebomb theory" is at all applicable to you, you have been living with open and infested wounds for quite some time now. You are applying Band-Aids to hemorrhages. You are taking aspirin when you need morphine. Your heart is hanging half out of its breast cavity and you wonder why it hurts so much to cry, or even to take a breath of fresh air. So do yourself, your husband, and everyone who truly loves and cares for you a favor and get yourself the only medicine that will begin to cure you: find your daughter!

@ *Why Search?* @

Date: Feb. 27 17:43 EST
Author: ElisaMB@aol.com
             Posted On America Online

Questions and answers prepared for a Live Chat, hosted by ElisaMB for the Adoption Forum of America Online. The chat topic: *Lending Support to Searching Birth Parents*. Author's note: While the following text refers solely to women, several searching birth fathers have written that all of it applies equally to men.

Q: Why would a birth mother ever want to search for her relinquished child?

A: While every original mother of a surrendered child has legally relinquished the right to parent that child, she never truly relinquishes her innate love, feelings of responsibility, or genuine, ongoing concern for the child's present and future welfare. Closed adoption in particular seeks to negate or to obliterate those feelings. A newly-bereaved birth mother will immediately begin to develop her own self-defense mechanisms in order to "forget," to convince herself that she is not in pain, or that her decision was in her child's best interests. But when each one of those superimposed or self-imposed mechanisms ceases to function, the birth mother's only other option is to discover the truth for herself. This usually means that she needs to find her relinquished child.

Q: What exactly do you mean by "lending support"? Isn't this illegal?

A: Until and unless the Uniform Adoption Act passes, it is not illegal to aid a birth mother to locate her surrendered child. Searching for an adopted child is not the same thing as contacting that child. Both processes need to be carried out with the utmost intelligence, sensitivity, and responsibility, most especially when the search or eventual contact involves a minor. You can lend your support by offering an open mind, a listening heart, a soft shoulder. Often the birth mother just needs to know that her good friends or family won't turn their backs on her if she proceeds with the search.

Q: Wouldn't it be easier and better for everyone concerned if the original parent would just wait for the adopted child to become an adult, before initiating a search?

A: Most adoptive parents feel this way, and many adult adoptees have expressed the concern that, had they been "found" (but they really mean "contacted") at a younger age, it would have made their adopted lives more difficult. But for the birth mother who needs to know whether her child is dead or alive, the suggestion that she continue to wait only heightens her growing sense of fear, frustration, sadness and anger.

Q: Other than alleviating these symptoms of the birth parent's grief, are there any other reasons why searching for an adoptee might be a good idea?

A: Yes, I can list numerous possible benefits of searching for a minor child:
1. It helps the original mother regain control of those areas of her life where she was once most vulnerable to loss. She will not regain custody of her surrendered child, but she will regain custody of herself as a mature, intelligent, capable and self-possessed woman.
2. It forces the original mother to deal with the reality of herself as a birth mother-for-life, to come out of the closet (at least with herself).
3. It enables her to accept the reality of her child as an adoptee-for-life, as a child raised by another mother, within a different environment, with a different set of values, etc.

4. It enables the integration of her past with her present and future: her two separate lives and identities can now begin to merge into one.

5. It often promotes or vastly accelerates the healing process.

6. Sharing the desire to find her surrendered child with her spouse can open up a mutually vital avenue of communication (or a can of worms!).

7. Likewise for close family, friends, and co-workers.

8. It helps her subsequent children to see her as a mother who "would have searched forever"; it reconfirms her unconditional love for each of her children.

9. Searching may help her to resolve issues of secondary infertility.

10. The search process can help resolve issues of anger and guilt towards the birth mother's parents, the birth father, social workers and anyone who had anything to do with the relinquishment decision.

11. Searching provides HOPE ("the thing with feathers" ~Emily Dickinson) for an eventual reunion. Alternatively, if the surrendering mother has found herself stuck living in the past, hope can lead her to pursue future goals.

12. By searching for her child when she chooses to, rather than when it is acceptable or prescribed by the present system, she helps to vanish the myth of "the light at the end of the tunnel" (the minute her surrendered child turns the magical age of eighteen).

13. As with families of MIAs, search is the only way of knowing for sure what has become of one's child.

14. The sooner she finds her child, the greater the amount of time she has, in preparation for a mutually desired reunion. Analogy: an amniocentesis at four-and-a-half months of gestation shows that the unborn child has Down Syndrome. The expectant parents can use the remaining half of the pregnancy to prepare themselves to be the best possible parents to their special-needs child.

15. The adopted child is spared the fears, confusion, doubt,

and anger of having to initiate the search himself. After all, if a child is lost, is it not ultimately the parent's responsibility to search for him, rather than the other way around?

Q: Are there any good reasons *not* to search for a child?

A: Yes. There is a flip side to each of the above-listed reasons.

Why Not Search?

1. It requires coming to terms with the fact that the relinquishment is a done deal; shedding all past secrecy and denial; dealing with guilt, shame, anger, sadness, etc. Being honest with oneself is rarely easy or fun.
2. It will eventually require coming out of the closet with those closest to you in your present life: your spouse or significant other; your subsequent children; close relatives; close friends and co-workers. Being honest with others is even harder and less amusing than being honest with oneself.
3. It may require a great deal of time, energy, money, patience, persistence, determination, and imagination; any or all of these resources and skills may not be readily available.

Q: Let's say a birth mother locates her minor-aged child. Now what?

A: Now comes the hardest part: 'Birth mother Limbo.' This is when the birth mother, and those who supported her throughout her search, need to muster all of their corporate intelligence, maturity, responsibility, and sensitivity, to prepare for the best possible reunion.

Q: But how does the birth mother determine when is the best time for contact?

A: I believe that the biological and spiritual ties between a birth parent and her surrendered child will be the best guide. Just as every reunion between adult adoptees and their family of origin is unique, there is no set rule of thumb for when or whether a birth parent should contact a minor child or his adoptive parents.

There are extreme cases where a minor-aged adoptee chooses to leave his adoptive home and move in with his family of origin. But for most birth mothers, this is not the scenario. She has to gather all the information she can about her child in order to determine whether, when and how it is best for her to contact her surrendered child. The better (not necessarily the longer) she "does time in Birthmother Limbo," the better she will know how and when to approach her surrendered child.

@ *Contacting Minors Directly* @

Date: July 28 11:47 AM EDT
From: Danya@american.edu
To: Adoption Triad Mailing List

If I had been contacted directly while I was a teenager, I would probably have fallen completely in love with my birth mother, and dreamed of escape from my adoptive mother, who would then have made my life a living hell. If my birth mother had contacted my adoptive mother while I was a minor, I am completely certain that she would have been threatened with legal action. It would have been ugly for both of us. My adoptive mom would have taken out her anger and jealousy on me.

To give you a little background, my adoptive mom was a classic stage mother. Basically our relationship was then, and is still now, all about control. She used all the guilt inherent in the "chosen child" story to pour her frustrated ambition into me. I was almost a child prodigy on the piano, and then I rebelled and dropped it when I was fifteen. I was almost valedictorian of my high school, but rebelled against that, too, my senior year.

Perhaps there is an analogy here to the experience of some of you birth mothers who became pregnant as a teenager. You were stuck in a situation only partially of your own making, and without enough control to handle it in the way that was best for you. If my birth mother had contacted me directly as a teenager, the situation would have been similar. I would have had all that emotion with which to deal, but without the control over my own life to protect myself. After all, having been raised the way I was, as an upper-class over-achiever, the threat of no car at night, or no college in the future, is a very scary thing. The adoptive parents have enormous control, and not knowing them, you cannot imagine how they will use that power.

I'm with Elisa—spying from a distance is a very good idea —just to get an idea of how your child relates to her adoptive parents. The earliest I could have handled contact would have been when I left home to attend college. I would have needed that physical separation from my adoptive parents.

Danya

@ *A Time and Place* @

Date: Sept. 27 22:25 EDT
From: ElisaMB@aol.com
To: *Maria@Indy.Net

Dear Maria, as the song goes, someday, somewhere, there will come a time and a place, for you and *Keith to grow together, if not as mother and son, then as something equally special.

By making yourself known now to your teenage son, you have given him two invaluable and precious gifts: time, and the knowledge of your love for him. Keith knows right now how much you have always loved him. He no longer needs to worry and wonder, or to feel angry or sad, abandoned or rejected, as is the case with many older adoptees whose birth parents never searched for them.

Peace, Maria, and as Leroy says in Michelle Shocked's wonderful song *Anchorage*: "Keep on rockin', girl!"

@ *Beethoven's Eighteenth Symphony* @

Date: Dec. 11 9:29 AM EDT
From: Maria@Indy.Net
To: Adoption Triad Mailing List

I have five days until Keith turns eighteen. (He and Beethoven share the same birthday.) I did something really wild last
week. I was in Keith's town buying a 1959 Fender Deluxe
tweed amplifier (rare and totally original electronics) at a guitar store I have known about since the first time I cruised
through town looking for the person that turned out to be
my son.

Last week I walk into this store, a man comes out of the back
and says "You're Maria *DeSanto, aren't you?" I said, "Yes!
How did you know?" He said he had just read the huge article in the local paper about our band playing with legendary
bluesman Yank Rachell the following Wednesday and he
saw my picture, remembered my husband's name from the
phone call about the amp. Connection!

So, I bought the amp for my husband. Everyone was ooing
and ahhing in the store because guitar players LOVE old
fender amps and lucky me, I got the sucker! I then asked the
guy if I could buy a gift certificate and if so, would the recipi-
ent have to spend it all in one purchase or what? The guy
said, "That depends. How much do you want to make this
out for?" I said, "A thousand dollars." He said, "Well, they can
spend it as slowly as they wish!" He then asked to whom he
should make out the gift certificate. I gulped and said, "Make
it out to Keith *Future." The guy looked at me and said, "I
know him!" I asked, "You do?" He then told me Keith had
taken guitar lessons at the store from their resident teacher,
beginning six years ago or so. He had just been in there buying strings, a week before I came in.

I told the store owner that I am Keith's birth mother and that the gift certificate was the best idea I had for my son's eighteenth birthday. I explained that I just don't know the kid and all I know is, if it were me, I would really love a huge gift certificate from a music store! So then everybody who works in the store got in the act and came over and started to tell me all they could think of about Keith! Then the guy who taught Keith guitar came in and everyone grabbed him and we were introduced! We talked about Keith and amps, guitars, pickups (I have the Eric Clapton setup on my '86 Stratocaster and so does the teacher!) The guitar teacher is a late '40s very cool, old hippie kind of guy. (I know! So am I. Old hippie gal, that is!) The place was buzzing like they were witnessing the start of some big Harmonic Conversion! I felt surrounded by people who truly cared that this thing should go down with good vibes. The guy who sold me the amp offered to hold the gift certificate in his desk and he gave me another one that I can mail to Keith in a company envelope, and just says there is a gift for him at this store and to see this particular guy.

Afterwards, I drove back to Indy in a torrential downpour and felt so powerful! We played our gig to a sold-out audience.

Hugs, Maria

@ *Break on Through* @

Date: Dec. 17 1:59 AM EDT
From: Maria@Indy.Net
To: Adoption Triad Mailing List

Is that Beethoven's Fifth I hear? I probably will vent about something if I don't hear from Keith soon, but I am just happy to know that he has made it to adulthood and that he is beautiful, and perfect, and talented, and stubborn, and wild and all the things that make him who he is!

Thanks for all of your support and loving, understanding posts throughout this tough time. It means everything, on some of those dark days when I feel so alone.

Yesterday was almost worse than today. Twenty-four hours ago, at the stroke of midnight, I was in tears. I swore I smelled alcohol and that Keith was getting drunk to celebrate his eighteenth birthday. I don't drink at all, never have, and yet I smelled whiskey somewhere in my brain. It was weird. So this morning I cranked up The Doors' Whiskey Bar song as loud as I could on my stereo, and danced around the house with all of my dogs and cats. My parakeet sang along and we had a great morning of cappuccino and Jim Morrison. I then sat around and waited for my phone to ring. It didn't. It WILL ring, though. . . . one of these days.

Love, Maria

@ *Stairway to Heaven* @

Date: Dec. 15, 6:57 PM EST
From: Sharon@aol.com
To: ElisaMB@aolcom

One of the reasons I have felt drawn to you, Elisa, is because of your precious son. You see, I have an uncle who is both physically and mentally challenged as well. Although the dynamics are very different, the love I have always felt for this special man fills my heart. I can't imagine my life without him.

My Uncle Emil is now eighty-six years old and, due to medical problems, is confined to a nursing home in upstate New York. He lived independently most of his life and was the love of the family. He was so kind and gentle, like a great big old well-worn teddy bear.

I remember the first time I took my children to visit him, when the boys were aged one, two and three. I had an appointment to get my hair cut. Uncle Emil asked if he could watch the boys for me so that I wouldn't have to drag them along to the hairdresser's. I put the children to bed for an afternoon nap and, without a moment's worry, went on my way.

When I returned, the boys were all sleeping like lambs and Uncle Emil was sitting on the stairs. He was so afraid that one of them might wake up and try to climb down the steps by himself and fall. Being from Florida, all one story houses, the boys were fascinated with the stairs and spent most of their time climbing up and down them. My darling Uncle had spent the entire two-and-a-half hours just sitting there!

What God takes away in mental ability, He more than compensates with other, sometimes more important, qualities, like a gentle spirit. The entire town knew my uncle and every-one kept an eye out for him. God help anyone who might ever try to take advantage of him!

Big Grin Hugs, Sharon

> Date: Dec. 15 8:46 PM EST
> From: ElisaMB@aol.com
> To: Sharon@aol.com

Dear Sharon,

If my son is still climbing *Jacob's Ladder* at the age of eighty-six, I hope to live to be one-hundred-and-seven . . . just so that I can watch my baby sitting on that *Stairway to Heaven.*

@ @ @ @ @ @ @ @

CHAPTER THREE

"Who is my mother?
And who are my siblings?"
(Matthew 12:48)

@ *Animal Adoption* @

Date: Aug. 23 11:27 AM EST
To: bmoms@abcd.edu
From: ElisaMB@aol.com

My youngest daughter Madeleine has been attending Zoo Camp at the Philadelphia Zoo for the past two weeks. Yesterday she came home with a special sticker which she wanted me to iron on to her Tee-shirt. It has a cute picture of a frog within a leopard within a rhinoceros, and a bird overhead. But underneath the picture stood the backwards word ADOPT, followed by other words, in smaller lettering, which I never bothered to read.

I said, "Maddie, I'd be happy to iron the sticker to your shirt, but let's cut off all the lettering first and just leave the picture of the animals, O.K.?" She asked me why, and while I fumbled around for an explanation, she looked at me, shrugged, and trotted off to find a pair of scissors.

This morning after I dropped her off at camp, I decided to take an early morning stroll through America's First Zoo, before the crowds began to arrive. I wandered by the kangaroo joeys, just freshly emerged from their mothers' pouches. Mother and father kangaroos were laying down resting next to their babies during the breakfast hour. Next to them, mother and daughter hippos waded side by side in their private pool, twirling their little round ears in unison. Next to them were a tapir, and then a rhinoceros, each with large signs posted in front of their exhibits proudly proclaiming: *I'm pregnant! Baby due October* and *Gestation period: 16 months.* After that, I went to visit the three white lion cubs which were born at the zoo in March and May of this year. There were two sister cubs and another female baby cousin, all happily cavorting with one another while we watched in awe and wonder at the naturalness of their play within this huge outdoor playpen. Across from the gorgeous lion babies was a newborn gorilla cling- ing to its mother's back. The father, aunts, and cousin gorillas were all curiously milling around the mother and her baby. Lastly, I visited another mother-daughter pair, an aard-vark and her fully-grown pink daughter, all curled up and asleep together.

How humane humans are to animals, especially when it comes to the issues of family preservation and adoption! And yet how inhumanely many human societies treat their own spe-cies in the same regard! It would never occur to a zoological society to rip a suckling infant away from its own mother in order to give it to an infertile mother of the same species.

Even the rare offspring born in captivity, such as the white lion cubs, which are destined to an animal jet-set life of tour-ing from one major zoo to another, are kept with their moth-ers and their fathers as long as possible. Thereafter, they are not separated from their siblings or from their cousins.

When I saw the word ADOPT, I already knew what the Zoo Adoption Program meant. When humans adopt a zoo animal, they give money to the zoo in order to provide food, shelter, and family togetherness for that animal. They give the true gift of life. They do not take the animal home. They do not pretend that it is their biological child.

I still owe my Madeleine an explanation for making her cut off the word ADOPT before agreeing to iron the sticker on to her Tee-shirt. Madeleine is the daughter who has always been the most upset about "giving her brother away to that other family."

@ *"Are You My Daddy?"* @

Date: July 14 2:59 PM EST
From: Danya@american.edu
To: Multiple recipients of Triad List

Following is one of the weirdest adoption stories I have heard, told to me by the adoptee herself:

Circa 1960, a young woman is married to a man who works as a chemist. There is much conflict about whether or not to have children. The husband and his parents are insistent that the couple have as many children as possible. The wife gives in, and they start trying to conceive a baby. Then, a tragic accident in the chemistry lab! The husband spills acid down the front of his body and is severely injured, including the parts needed for reproduction. In the back of her mind, the wife thinks, "Whew, no kids." But the pressure from the husband's family does not let up, and after a while, the wife agrees to conceive through artificial insemination by donor. This was an exorbitantly expensive procedure at the time.

While the wife was pregnant, her husband was killed in a horrible car accident. After the baby, a daughter, was born, the paternal grandparents said, "That baby is not related to us. We don't want anything to do with her." The mother wasn't prepared for any of this, and she surrendered her daughter for adoption.

Quite a story, huh? It really got me thinking about the whole idea of anonymous donor insemination. Personally, I would like to see it outlawed. I have actually gone head-to-head with lesbian friends about this, because I think that any child deserves to know the identity of his or her father.

If a woman is single, or married to an infertile man, or a lesbian, tough shit—get a friend to donate his sperm, or adopt a truly needy child. I am developing a serious distaste for people who think that they *deserve* a little carbon copy of themselves, without any strings attached.

I don't care if the insemination company does "genetic counseling," or takes pages of information on the sperm donor daddy. The human beings who are the product of this practice have a right to know who their father is. Period.

Danya

@ *Rejection, Secrecy, Survival* @

Date: Dec. 2 4:58 AM EDT
From: *Celeste@eeyore.edu
To: Multiple recipients of Triad list

How I wish I had some magic response that would make you understand why your birth mother refuses to meet you. I think your birth mom split off from herself in order to survive. Her rejection is not so much of you but a rejection of her former self. The former self no longer exists to welcome you. You didn't ask to be born. How can anyone hate an infant, much less his or her own?

I am a birth mother who has been rejected these last one-and-one-half years by my found birth son. I know what a devastating experience this has been for me. I've heard that rejection is even worse for an adoptee. It is out of affiliation with your pain that I feel compelled to give you my very best explanations for rejection:

1. *Family secrecy:* I have met birth mothers who have lost marriages over this. For most, it was not so much the fact that their husbands learned that they had married "damaged goods." Rather, it has been a question of trust. Imagine being married to someone for 28 years to learn that they've kept secret the fact that he or she has another child somewhere. This can be as devastating to trust as an extra-marital affair. The longer the secret is kept, the harder it becomes to tell. It is no little secret. It can, and does, break up marriages.

Telling my subsequent children has actually improved my relationship with one of my sons. He is quite relieved to hear that his mother is not perfect. The other, however, has become distanced from me due to the revelation. I try to draw him out but it is not easy. He is old enough to know that there was another man before his beloved father. He is old enough to reel from the idea that he is not my firstborn. He is old enough to feel that somehow I "got rid of" his inconvenient half-brother. I am having a very difficult time explaining this to an omnipotent teen-ager. I've already lost one son. I simply don't have another to lose.

2. *Societal secrecy:* Closed records reinforce the idea that what birth parents have done is so heinous that it must be forever concealed. Getting carried away with my first love became a vile and unspeakable act. The fact that I was kicked out of my Catholic school, removed from my home, and denied the presence of my lover to give birth in pain and isolation, was nothing compared to the messages I was given after the fact.

After I relinquished my son, I initially felt an increase in self-esteem. I'd made a thoughtful and mature decision and handled a crisis pregnancy in a way I had thought was best for my son. It didn't take long, however, for society to knock the props out from under me again. It soon began to sink in that giving my son up for adoption was nothing short of social infanticide. Therefore, I learned to shut up about it.

3. *Emotional survival:* Relinquishment strikes at so much of what is the definition of womanhood. It strikes at our femininity, our sexuality, our reputations, our maternal instincts, our sense of family, our sense of care-giving, our emotional instincts, etc., ad infinitum. Not many women can carry a child for nine months, feel it kicking and growing inside, give birth to it, and then relinquish it, without making that baby into a "non-person." The human mind can only take so much, and then it somehow snaps!

Relinquishment is not unlike participating in the death of a loved one. I held my son in my seventeen-year-old arms and instead of feeling empowered, I felt even younger and less capable. After nine months of hormonal upheaval, after a complete physical reformation, after a complete social change, after the agony of childbirth, I heaved myself up on my elbows to see what it all was for. I knew in that instant that I would kill for my infant, and yet I could not have him. I relinquished him believing that he would be better off with someone else. This is no less delusional than the birth mom who performs an "emotional abortion," after the fact.

I've been asking "Why?" for two years. In that time, I've received many kind and thoughtful responses. I've recently become aware that I've been asking for logical answers when what I've really sought has been some sort of appeasement for my disturbing emotions. Those are two very different things. Emotions are not logical or rational. They have a life of their own. You can do all the logical investigation you want but at some point, the search will lead you inward. I'm doing better now that I've learned to narrow my search. I wish you the best of luck in yours.

Celeste

@ *The Smell of Belonging* @

Date: July 31 10:13 AM EST
From: ElisaMB@aol.com
To: bmoms@abcd.edu

A recently reunited birth mother wrote: «Twenty-eight years later, we smelled familiar to each other!»

I remember attending the first C.U.B. retreat in Maryland a few years ago. We were all staying together at a cozy little mountain-top conference center. It was a good opportunity for all of us to get to know one another pretty well. I found myself drawn like a magnet to each of the reunited mother-and-child pairs. I marveled at the incredible ease, familiarity, and physical resemblance between the mother and her adult son or daughter.

One particular workshop attracted every single reunited pair. The topic had to do with adoptees and their feelings, many years after the fact. I sat silently in the back corner of the room, listening to one story after another. First the adoptee would say something and then his or her mother would say something. They were all saying the same thing! They were talking about smells! They were each saying that they could tell they *belonged* to the other, the minute they first embraced, by their *noses!* All their fears melted away just by smelling their long-lost mother or child.

I have never forgotten the smell of my firstborn. It was there again in my next four baby girls. I smell it every time I kiss them in bed late at night, as they are dreaming. I dream of smelling it again in my son's hair some day . . . and to allow him the reciprocal feeling of belonging.

@ *Synchronicity* @

Date: Jan 6 9:59 AM EDT
From: ElisaMB@aol.com
To: Multiple recipients of Triad list

I agree with birth father Saul's theory that family members separated unnaturally from one another since birth inevitably find a way of reconnecting. If the five senses won't permit the connection, then the sixth sense begins to kick in. Even among family members who see one another regularly, there are all sorts of psychic synchronicities. For example, I usually know by the sound of the phone when it's my mother calling.

People who lose one of their five senses generally acquire greater acuteness among the other four senses, in addition to developing the sixth sense. A blind person's hearing is often much better than a seeing person's; a deaf person often has remarkable eyesight as well as insight.

Thus it makes utter sense to me that an adoptee or an original parent, when robbed of any way to connect with his loved one through one of the five natural senses, will develop a supernatural sensitivity as a replacement.

@ *Mother of Three* @

Date: Nov. 20 11:41 PM EDT
From: Joan@aol.com
To: bmoms@abcd.edu

Dear friends, I just can't believe my good fortune as it continues. Finding my daughter so easily through the reunion registry, and finding a daughter who is such a lovely, sensitive, caring and warm person. Pinch, pinch, knock on wood. One of the great things about all this is that, finally, I am beginning to believe that it is all true, that she is in my life, and that she will stay there. I think I have been waiting eight months for the other shoe to drop, for her to say, well, thanks for the information I needed, I know where I came from, so bye-bye. That is not going to happen.

Our second meeting yesterday was in L.A. On the way there, my eleven-year-old remarked a couple of times that it seemed very weird that this was only our second in-person meeting, it seemed much more frequent than that, and we all agreed. It seems like we've been a family forever.

We met her at the restaurant where she has worked for six years. The passion in her life right now is dancing, and working as a waitress gives her flexibility for going to classes and auditions, and money to live on while she pursues her career. The restaurant is spectacular. The building is new but was built to appear old, elegant and full of ambiance. *Karly is very well liked by everyone there.

My daughter was waiting for us with her best friend since middle school, *Carly, also a dancer. They look and act like sisters; they are beautiful and vibrant. Hugs all around. I am introduced to Carly and to everyone else who stops by as "my birth mom." I can feel everyone staring at me, looking for any resemblance, I'm sure. I have brownish hair with a lot of red highlights; my daughter is a total redhead. We have pale skin and matching freckles. She has an unusual mouth, her father's. My eyes are hazel; hers are true green.

There was one moment when Carly turned to my Karly and said, "Your mom said we have the same laugh." I waited for the awkward pause or the correction. There was none. Finally, acknowledgment. The words "your mom" are echoing in my ears. I am no longer the person who gave birth to an unknown, fantasy bundle in a blanket and wondered for 25 years if she was dead or alive. I am no longer the mother of two children. I am seated at a table surrounded by my three children. The acknowledgment has made us a family of five. It's real.

The other Carly left, we had a great lunch, talked about lots of things. Little comments gave me glimpses into her unknown life. "I used to . . ." "On holidays, we usually . . ." She would talk about her cousins and about her other relatives. I wanted to say, "You're wrong. Your cousins are so-and-so; your aunts are my sisters. You only have one uncle. . . ."

Afterwards we walked through a park, took a lot of pictures, spent a little while at a museum. We passed a couple who asked for change for a dollar for the parking meter. They could be identified as Only in California. The man was probably mid-sixties and he reminded my youngest of a leprechaun. He was truly unique. Only his feet were not green; they were bright orange, beaded and turned up at the toes. (Really!) He wore lots of beaded clothing and some kind of sash. His female companion was about a foot-and-a-half taller, serene while he was effervescent. Both never stopped smiling. They thanked us for the quarters as if we had given them the shirts off our backs. He looked at my husband and said,

"Your wife has produced three beautiful children, yes?" An innocent remark from a funny little man, and I want to kiss him because he has made my day.

The day flew by. We went to the Santa Monica Beach. The weather was perfect: no smog; the sun was out; not even too cold. We walked on the pier eating cotton candy and feeding popcorn to the seagulls. We talked, we laughed, we took pictures and wrapped arms around one other. We saw a great show under the tent. We were a family. No, we are a family.

Love, Joan

@ *My Mother Liked to Tap Dance* @

Date: Jan. 27 10:34 AM EDT
From: Janet@uga.edu
To: ElisaMB@aol.com

Dear Elisa, I got a call this evening from the confidential intermediary who, after a lot of hullabaloo, is handling my search. He told me some basic facts. Not only was it stuff about which I had no idea, but it was very comforting. Like, at the time of my birth, my mother's hobbies were sewing, cooking, knitting, ballet, and tap dancing.

Tap dancing! I've never had a dance lesson of any kind in my life, though I love to go to discos. It's silly, but I am thrilled to know this little tidbit of information. The "shadow woman" doesn't have a face yet, but she now has a height and weight, hair color and eye color, and hobbies. I don't know, tap dancing says funny and irreverent to me. I have been so worried about rejection, and I still don't know anything. But tap dancing makes me hopeful.

Love, Janet

Subj.:   Re: My mother liked to tap dance!
Date: Jan 27 10:33 PM EDT
From: ElisaMB@aol.com
To: Janet@uga.edu

Dearest Janet: The Princess of Wales likes to tap dance, and despite a horrible marriage, the poor darling is an excellent mother! So keep that thought tapping under your shoe.

Cheers, Elisa

@ *Today My Mother Became Real* @

Date: Dec. 19 3:28 AM EDT
From: *Claire@parseley.com
To: Multiple recipients of Triad list

Yesterday, my mother did not have a name. Today, she does.

I spoke on the phone with a searcher who was able to give me her real name, her address, phone number, place of work, her other two daughter's names, and a lot more information that I ever thought I would have.

Someone tell me I am not crazy! The first emotion I felt after I got off the phone was very intense anger! I found out that she lives so close to me; she was born close to me; she lived within twenty miles of me when I was growing up! It made me so angry to know that she's been so close all this time. My adoptive mother told me she lived on the east coast.

So now I have to decide how to contact her. I don't think I should until after Christmas. I don't know if I can call her on the phone, I don't think I can wait for her to respond to a letter. I have no idea what I will do.

Confusedly yours, Claire

Subj.: Re: Today my Mother became real
Date: Dec. 19 10:18 AM EDT
From: ElisaMB@aol.com
To: Multiple recipients of Triad list

Dearest Claire! I would embrace that anger, or at least I understand it and it makes me want to embrace you for feeling it! Your original mother should understand it, too, if you will only try to explain it to her yourself. The analogy I would use is this: a mother whose kid has run away is worried sick over that child. She calls 911 and missing persons, is convinced the kid has been kidnapped or run over by a truck. The police conduct a citywide search which yields nothing. The kid has been at a friend's house watching one rental movie after another and has no idea that he is even missed. When the kid finally goes home, the mother wants to kill him.

I did something like that when I was five years old. I got angry at my parents for something and just took off after dinner without telling them. I went to visit a little old lady who baby-sat in the same apartment complex. I played with the baby and then we sat and watched TV and ate graham crackers for hours, while my parents and the police and all the neighbors were all over the place outside with flashlights looking for my dead body. The little old lady assumed my parents knew where I was. After "Seventy-Seven Sunset Strip" and the late news, I decided it was time to go home, and I was greeted by all those searchers. My mother cried tears of joy and anger when she saw me.

Your confusion is so natural and normal, Claire. However and whenever you decide to contact your mother, I pray that she will understand that your emotions are based in love.

Elisa

@ *An Adoptee's Impossible Dream* @

Date: Aug. 28 11:40 AM EDT
From: ElisaMB@aol.com
To: *Marcy@cruzio.com

Dear Marcy: I was delighted to hear you sing your "Adoption Song" on stage at the Philadelphia Folk Festival last night. I had heard it and your interview previously on the radio, but had forgotten it was you. It is the morning after the festival, as I listen to WXPN and think about your words to me last night: "My records are sealed. I have no names. It may be impossible to find my birth family . . ."

It is not impossible, Marcy. With her permission, I'd like to share how the impossible dream recently came true for Danya, an adoptee whose search for her original family seemed as hopeless as your own: sealed records, no name, only her place and date of birth. Danya had registered with every conceivable reunion registry and had searched for years on her own, to no avail. Finally she was referred to a private investigator.

Following is an e-mail journal of Danya's search:

Subj.: My Search
Date: Aug. 2 12:43 PM EST
From: Danya@american.edu
To: ElisaMB@aol.com

Elisa, now that I've decided, I am suddenly incredibly impatient! I want to find my birth mother IMMEDIATELY. I think you are so right not to postpone this any further. I sat down and tried to figure out how much more screwed up I could get by finding my mother right now, and realized I was already about as screwed up as I could get! I suppose that only time will tell though—so let's hope it's soon.

****

Subj.: Search is a go!
Date: Aug. 4 4:28 PM EST
From: Danya@american.edu
To: Multiple recipients of Triad list

Hi all. I am SO excited! I am about to mail off the contract to *Caroline to search for my birth mother!!!!! Keep your hats on ladies and gents, I will definitely be coming to you to ask for tips about THE CONTACT. I want to call, but I guess I should try to keep my hopes down until I find out that she hasn't fallen off the face of the earth.

****

Subj.: She's been found!!!!
Date: Aug. 15 1:35 PM EST
From: Danya@american.edu
To: Multiple recipients of Triad list

Caroline called me this morning! MY BIRTH MOTHER IS FOUND!!! She's alive and well (thank God!!) and I will be calling her this weekend!!! I'm so happy I could just scream! I keep telling myself to be prepared for the worst, but just knowing that she is found and reachable feels so amazing. My biggest fear has been that she dropped off the face of the earth somehow. And Caroline was amazingly fast—she got my information on Friday and called today! I'm freaking out my co-workers with my big, unexplained smile. :) :) :) :) :) :) :) :) :) :) :) :) :) :) :) :) Danya

****

Subj.:   Danya's reunion :)
Date: Aug. 18 7:47 PM EST
From: Danya@american.edu
To: Multiple recipients of Triad list

Happy Friday, everyone! I don't think I'm back down on earth yet, so the graphic blow-by-blow will have to wait. I called my MOM for the first time last night, and it was an absolute fantasy reunion!!!

When I started into the "is this a good time to talk" lines, she started quizzing me on who I was. When I told her that I was an adoptee born on . . . etc., she started crying and the first thing she said was, "I've been waiting for you to call." :) :) :) :) So of course I lost it too and we both just cried for a while. It was so amazing.

*Katherine (wow! her name!) never married or had any other children, and had been hoping I would call her someday. She wants me in her life! She sounds like me and laughs like me! Her sister and father both want to meet me too. She is absolutely everything I could ever hope for. She is loving and funny and wise. She has had a really interesting life and has a great job. Not only is she everything I could ask for in a birth mother, I think we are going to be amazing friends. We have so many interests in common, and similar liberal/radical political leanings. And she has a Ph.D. in political science and taught college for a few years, which is my career goal!!! I am going to visit over labor day weekend. She lives about 15 minutes away from my adoptive parents—in the school district I attended!!

Katherine called me this morning, just to wish me a good morning, and to make sure I was real. I was so glad she called, because I wasn't sure that she was real, either. :) I sent pictures this morning. Not only have I discovered my "other identity," but I've fallen completely in love!

The best advice in the "How to Make Contact" letter is to follow your heart when it comes to calling vs. writing. I called almost immediately, and I think my birth mother is as impulsive and sensitive as I am. Hearing one another's voices was so important.

* *

Subj.:   REUNION: Danya's happy one
Date: Aug. 20 9:01 PM EST
From: Danya@american.edu
To: Multiple recipients of Triad list

After getting a full page of information on my birth mother, grandfather, and an aunt from the P.I., I promptly ignored her advice to sleep on it and called later that night. She has been hoping I'd contact her since I turned 18, and of course had no idea how difficult it had been. When it came out much later that I had hired a P.I., she started crying again, saying that she was elated that I wanted to get in touch with her that badly.

I was conceived on the Fourth of July, right after Katherine graduated from high school. My father was her high school sweetheart. She hasn't told me his name yet, but I have a feeling that she will try to contact him for me if I ask—she has been so incredibly open! He has a wife and kids, so there are some half-siblings out there. I will be as patient as it takes.

She asked me a ton of questions about growing up, and seemed so happy and relieved that I had a happy childhood and was doing well now. She SOUNDS like me and laughs JUST like me. I couldn't believe it!

Right after I got off the phone Thursday night I felt like a whole and complete person for the first time in my life. I think this is going to be one of the most significant relationships in my life and I am SO HAPPY there just aren't words!

Elisa—Keep your chin up. No matter how long it takes, I know your son will be as thrilled as I am to have another loving mother in his life. :)

Danya

@ *Breaking the Iceberg* @

Date: Sept. 19 1:21 PM EDT
From: ElisaMB@aol.com
To: Danya@american.edu

Danya, your birth father sent you his resume and a topographical map? I love it! Both of your birth parents sound absolutely delightful. Be sure to point out to your birth dad that he now has an even greater accomplishment to add to his curriculum vitae: having produced you!

One persistent difficult thought occurs to me regarding your budding relationship with each of them: if it were I who was just now facing the harsh reality of losing you, I would feel devastated! Here you have a mother, a father, and their offspring; all three of you not only genetically related but also highly intelligent, well-educated, caring, sensitive, success-bound . . . What a beautiful family you could have been! What a senseless, stupid loss.

You asked for suggestions for "ice-breakers" between yourself and Katherine. Consider your reunion an iceberg, buried nine-tenths beneath the surface. You have a lot of ice to break. And give your birth father the biggest break of all, Danya: I think you're both going to adore one another. You and he sound even more alike than you and your birth mother.

@ *Danya's "Sperm Donor"* @

Date: Sept. 21 1:21 PM EDT
From: Danya@american.edu
To: Multiple recipients of Triad list

First, I want to point out that my use of the description "sperm donor" is fully tongue-in-cheek. Now let me tell you about my weekend with *David, my more-than-sperm-donor birth father! ;)

I was completely blown away because HE LOOKS JUST LIKE ME!!!! :) :) :) My birth mother really doesn't look like me, and now I know why—almost all of my physical characteristics come from my birth father! It was so bizarre—we just stared and stared at each other. I have some pretty distinctive family features, like the big nose!

Too amazing. I had no idea how much I had missed knowing other people who look like me until I actually met one!!!! He was definitely blown away also, because his only other child, a son, takes after his mother's family and doesn't look much like him at all. If he ever had any doubts . . . ;)

It was a very different type of reunion than I had with my birth mother, because the two of us sat down in good scientist fashion and catalogued it. Katherine is much more like me in personality, very verbal and emotionally open, so we talked endlessly about our feelings and hopes. With David it was more of a cataloguing of similarities—every once in a while he would ask me something about myself, and always it was the same as him. Wow. One good thing is that it seems that I have inherited his faster metabolism and skinny tendencies —he has no sweet tooth and a taste for simple foods like plain vegetables, just like me, whereas Katherine is a total sugar junkie and has followed all the women of her family into a pudgy middle age. David is small and very fit for a guy heading for fifty. Of course, he is a professional outdoorsman, so that helps. One of the only physical traits I have gotten from Katherine is her lousy eyesight. Arg.

We were laughing about the topographical map, and I pointed out that I can read them, which many people cannot—definitely inherited. He said that they take all their prospective geology majors out on a "field study" their first semester, which the students don't realize is actually a test to see if they have the spatial reasoning ability to make it as a geologist. I've always had uncanny spatial reasoning ability—testing in the 99th percentile nationally when I was in the 5th grade. The other amazing thing is that my musical talent comes from him—just like me he was good enough in high school to have been encouraged to go on as a career, but did not have the ear to be one of the best, so why bother? Wow. It turns out that his paternal grandfather originally immigrated to the US from Germany before W.W.I to play for the Boston Symphony. And as my psychologist mother-in-law confirms, musical ability has been largely proven to be an inherited trait.

Katherine and I share much more complicated abstract tendencies, like the need to analyze things TO DEATH, so we end up in some amazingly circular conversations. My last two conversations with her were great though. We really got into some emotional nitty-gritty and she is realizing that she can't mother me the way she wants to because I'm not a kid anymore. And just like me, she is a verbal perfectionist who polishes letters for days and constantly qualifies herself in conversation—which can add up to a communications problem.

As for my future relationship with David, we will have to see. He's not a real emotional guy, and I don't expect to ever get direct hints as to what sort of relationship he wants with me. He did ask us to come back any time, and seemed to really enjoy my company (I was on my best behavior ;). His wife was also very welcoming and hospitable, but also no directly stated input whatsoever from her. So I think I'll write him a very nice thank-you letter and directly state my low-key expectations. I really will leave it up to him whether he tells any of his extended family about me—he has one sister who they see occasionally, and a brother with whom they are not in touch—his parents are both dead.

My half brother is a more difficult subject. They say that they will tell him, but want to tell him in person, and are not sure when that will be. I'm perfectly happy being patient for a few years, but I really hope they do tell him, because I don't think I can resist contacting him in the long run. As Katherine said to me, I might be the next one to get a phone call out of the blue. :) He is only one year younger than me, so is long out of the house and lives on the west coast. He told them that he might swing by in January. Yikes. My husband and I stayed in his bedroom this weekend, and the wild thing is that we were both into science fiction and fantasy in high school and I have read EVERY SINGLE BOOK in his book case. Wow.

David's wife did tell me one neat thing—that he has talked about me over the years, wondering how I was and what I was up to. That is so great to hear!

@ *Call Me "Mom"* @

Date: Sept. 7 11:21 AM EDT
From: Judy@uvm.edu
To: Multiple recipients of Triad list

Danya, congratulations on your reunion! Some of the issues
you raised bring to mind some issues in my own reunion
which I'd like to address.

Danya wrote: «Having had just one reunion experience, I can
understand why an adoptee would be reluctant to bring up
her childhood to her birth mother a lot. Since Katherine and I
had our first, cover-two-entire-lives-in-one-day session, I did
tell her quite a bit. But I felt guilty about it somehow. Like it
was a slap in the face to detail all the things she couldn't do
for me as I was growing up.»

As most of you may recall, my own reunion is now over two
years old, with the face to face meeting just about at the one
year mark. Not much has changed over the last two years.
But what Danya says about being reluctant to bring up her
childhood must be common for adoptees. I know many of us
have hoped and prayed we would finally get the whole picture about our children from babyhood through adulthood,
yet for whatever reasons it doesn't happen. For me personally, I take it as more of a "slap in the face" NOT to hear about
all these details from my son. As birth mothers, we have many
regrets about not being there during these times, but my son's
holding back the details makes me think something was wrong
in his adoptive family that he can't talk about. I would welcome his childhood stories, his dreams and his aspirations
and what life was like for him with his family.

Danya, would detailing your life with your adoptive family
in some way make you feel disloyal to them? Most birth
mothers I know would welcome the details.

Danya wrote: «What other words for "mother" are there? My adoptive mom will always be Mom, but I really want to call Katherine something that acknowledges her relation to me. For those who are reunited, what do your adoptee-kids call you?»

The name is another issue in the relationship that causes some pain for me. I envy the birthmoms whose children want to call them Mom. We can't ever be the Mom they had in the parenting sense, but we are Mom in many other ways. For my son to call me 'Judy' signals to me that there's a wall he has erected between us, and a space he needs to maintain to prevent too much closeness or acceptance of who I am in relationship to him. This is just my personal interpretation, but that's how it feels to me. I would never think of him anything other than my son, how can I be anything other than his Mom? My heart would jump out of my chest if he were able to call me 'Mom.' Once during a phone conversation he said it felt weird to refer to his adoptive parents as his parents to me, but I reassured him that that was fine; after all, they were.

Danya wrote: «I hope I am not overwhelming you all with my happy reunion stories. There has been a great deal of pain shared on this list recently, and I feel a genuine sorrow for all the agony that adoption has caused in many of our lives. I know that Katherine has suffered and grieved my loss a great deal. But I have to believe that with love and understanding, and a good bit of luck, we can all heal ourselves, and help heal each other.»

It's wonderful to hear your happy reunion story. It gives me hope as I move beyond the grief and loss I experienced. And your optimism sheds light on the darkness that still lingers for some. We can heal together.

Love, Judy in Vermont

@ *The Original Unmother* @

Date: Sept. 22 6:58 PM EDT
From: ElisaMB@aol.com
To: Multiple recipients of Triad List

Danya writes: «I really wish that my birth mother had had other children—she seems to have completely absorbed the "bad mother" verdict, and that low self-esteem has taken over her entire life. What do you b-moms think about the differences between those without other children and those with? Do those without other children feel the sting of being labeled a bad mother more than those that have other children?»

An objective observer who had no idea that I am a birth mother would call me a "good mother." But those who know me best, such as my husband and my daughters, know better. They know that I have always felt like an impostor, like the original unmother.

Many birth mothers tend to try to compensate for the mistake of surrendering a child every bit as much as some adoptive mothers try to compensate for their infertility. Birth mothers vacillate between two extremes: either they compensate by having as many "replacement babies" as soon as possible, or they don't have another baby for a long, long, time, sometimes never, after the surrender of their child. Either of these two post-surrender child-bearing decisions will reflect the birth mother's feelings about her unmotherhood.

The most important consideration, Danya, is that Katherine never got a chance to be a mother, to you or to any child, after she first became one! That is bound to have a profound effect on your reunion. She has had only you, the phantom child, in whom to invest all of her motherly emotions, fears, hopes, dreams, and fantasies. When she gave birth to you, she became your mother. But because she has never been able to mother you, she has had to repress all of those motherly instincts.

When you become a mother yourself, you will see how an unmother's body refuses to deny her motherhood. Her breast-milk still begins to flow whenever you cry in the hospital newborn nursery or in your new mother's arms. Long after you were gone, and her milk had dried up, you were still that ghost baby out there somewhere, that amputated limb, and she felt the pain of your absence more often than on just your birthdays. . . .

I don't believe it is entirely possible to regain what has been lost in adoption. Even the best of reunion relationships, as many of you have asserted, can only hope to approximate the natural parent/child relationship which would have otherwise developed.

Losing my firstborn to adoption has broken me, like a fine porcelain vase, into a zillion shards. It's going to take the rest of my life to find and glue all those pieces together again. But even then, I will never be the same mother, "good" or "bad," to any of my children, that I would have been, had I mothered each one of my babies.

@ *My Children's Mothers* @

Date: Oct. 14 12:38 AM EDT
From: *Mimi@aol.com
To: Multiple recipients of Triad list

I sometimes think there is something wrong with me because, so seldom is there a day when I don't think of my adopted children's original mothers. I have always felt guilty that my joy came from their pain.

My oldest is *Ned, born Jorge Garcia. His mother is *Marisa. She had a physical impairment which prevented her signing her name with anything but an "X." She came into a clinic, gave birth, and left. I have her ID number, the Colombian equivalent of our social security number. I have always had a gut feeling that Ned is a twin: little clues were dropped; outright questions denied.

I do feel there is a strong bond between mothers and children which is not broken by adoption. When Ned was in second grade, he cried nightly for his Colombian mother. I will always wonder what was going on with Marisa in that year. I assured Ned that Marisa loved him. I contacted the agency in Colombia, but they wouldn't help me to locate her. I hope and pray we can find her.

*Amy Kathleen is my daughter. Her original mother was *Mary Kathleen. We knew her mother was a high school student but, beyond that, we knew very little. We were given the classic lines, to quote the agency: "The baby's mother expressed much love and concern for the baby, as did her parents. She felt it was important for a child to be raised by two parents, by a mother and father who love one another and who can offer that security to a growing child. She realized the difficulties she and the child would experience if she kept her and tried to raise her alone in our society today."

When Amy was fifteen, I searched for Mary at my daughter's request. Mary had been killed in a car accident at age twenty-four, when Amy was seven. She had not had any other children.

Amy and I had a reunion this summer with Mary's parents and five siblings. We all get along very well. We have a photo album full of Mary's photos. Amy wears her class ring, sleeps with a stuffed animal Mary bought her but wasn't allowed to give her. Mary had a premonition of death so she left a letter with her trusted brother to give to her daughter should anything happen to her. Amy now has that letter.

My youngest is *Armand, born Armando Pineda, son of Elena. Elena wanted very much to keep him, but again felt she had no choice. It is very difficult to be a single mother in a country which offers no social or support programs. Women are treated more like property. Armand's mother is a maid, one of the lucky ones, as her employees are not Colombian, so she has better working conditions than if she worked for wealthy Colombians. She supports her family back home in a small mountain village. Colombian society is actually quite racist; the darker your skin, the more difficult your life. And she knew her baby would be dark. A dark-skinned male child has so little hope there. She delivered her baby in a hospital. Mothers share beds in large wards: one mother with her head at the top of the bed; the other mother with her head at the foot of the bed. Babies sleep in the bed with their mothers. Mothers breast-feed or the babies either don't get fed or get dysentery from improperly prepared formula. I don't know what the medical complication was, but Elena had to stay seven days in the hospital, an almost unheard-of length of stay. She nursed her son that whole time! I cannot even imagine her pain at saying good-bye to him.

Peace, Mimi

@ *Turtle Soup* @

Date: Aug. 17 6:41 PM EDT
From: Michele@aol.com
To: ElisaMB@aol.com

We are at an upscale pasta restaurant in Austin, Texas, enjoying a wonderfully creative dinner when Greg, just in the manner of conversation, says, "They used to call me a turtle when I was little. I was always so quiet and so slow."

I practically faint. I'm not sure why. I just remember seeing a turtle stuffed animal next to my hospital bed after my first son was born. The vision of the turtle has been bothering me since I started to remember the events surrounding Greg's birth. The stuffed animal makes me angry. Who brought it to me? Why are they bringing me a child's toy? Why are they treating me like a child? (Oh, cut them some slack. No one knows quite how to treat me, the mother/child.)

I can't sleep that night, as I need to connect with that damned turtle comment. Then I remember writing love letters to Ron (my high school sweetheart and Greg's birth dad) and drawing a little turtle after my signature. Now I can clearly see the turtle drawing. Yes, I was his little turtle. Because I was so quiet and so slow. And it was Ron who brought me the turtle in the hospital. Also, before this, I wasn't quite sure if I had, in fact, written Ron love letters. But now I know I did. Because I drew that turtle so many times.

I tell Greg about the love letters and the turtle sketches. He seems touched that his birth father's pet name for me was the same as a pet name his parents had for him. I don't tell him how I cried myself to sleep that night when all the pieces fell together. I don't mention how angry I am that it took twenty-five years for these similarities to become apparent, and that these two little turtles should have stayed together, both so quiet and so slow.

The next day, we are floating down a lazy river in San Marcos, all in our own little tubes, when Ian shouts, "Oh Mom, look! How cute! A mommy turtle and her baby!" Sure enough, on a rock jutting out of the lily pads, there was a proud momma turtle sunning herself with her little one on her back. I glance at Greg, who has a somewhat anxious look in his eye, and he seems to begin to paddle towards the turtle. But the current picks up and we all get swept away. It all happened so fast. We continued to float down the river.

I ponder that I am still quiet and slow. Greg is still quiet but is no longer slow. But this float down the river is nice and easy and we can all take life slowly this afternoon. We never mention the turtle again.

I'm in a gift shop, looking for souvenirs, and I stumble across a little ceramic turtle wearing a sailor hat. So I buy two; one for my Christmas tree and the other to carefully slip deep into my sailor son's backpack, waiting to be found, after we leave this vacation.

So that's how my most recent visit with my birth son Greg went: tender moments; tears; unspoken words; uncanny coincidences. All mixed together, like turtle soup.

Michele

@ *Scarred for Life* @

Date: April 1 5:52 PM EDT
From: Joan@aol.com
To: ElisaMB@aol.com

I learned many things yesterday during my fourth visit with my daughter Karly, but one thing above all else had the greatest impact.

She was talking in a way that showed me many of the insecurities she has. I was getting a look at the whole picture. The conversation was about how her ex-boyfriend had not tuned in to her feelings, that he had not enhanced her own view of herself, body image being just a small part of it. One of the things she dislikes most (besides the freckles that I and my other two kids have) is a large (about the size of a half-dollar) round brown birthmark on one of her breasts. I was driving while she talked. I think my mouth dropped open and the first thing I said was, "I didn't know you have a birthmark."

I haven't been able to stop thinking about that. I SHOULD KNOW she has a birthmark! I hate that I didn't know that! I hate that it took twenty-six years to know that! That one mark shows me that there are millions of things I don't know about my own daughter, and that I will never know. I feel very cheated, that I wasn't the first to see that mark, and that I have never seen it.

Joan

@ *Hibernation* @

Date: Aug. 17 10:40 AM EDT
From: ElisaMB@aol.com
To: Michele@aol.com

Michele, your turtles hit home with me. I am anything but quiet and slow, but I've always had a fascination with turtles. As a child, teenager, and college student, I nurtured any variety available: diamondback terrapins, Amazon side-necked turtles; musks; Japanese box turtles. Most recently we had two Eastern box turtles, gifts for my youngest daughter Madeleine.

More powerful and more telling than any other adoption- or motherhood-related-dreams, were my "bad turtle dreams." I have been plagued with them at every juncture of semi-conscious despair. My turtles would begin to uncontrollably and spontaneously multiply! The creatures I most loved for their peaceful, contained, slow, quiet natures became terrifying omnivorous sea-monsters of a furious population explosion in my own backyard swimming pool!

Over a two-week period of time last winter, away from my daughters and from Maddie's sick box turtle, I fully expected to have bad turtle dreams every night. Instead, for the first time, I dreamt of a beautifully cultivated pond, inhabited by lovely, peaceful turtles, living out their contented amphibious existence.

The first box turtle died while I was away. I replaced him with Valentine, who disappeared into our backyard the first day Maddie put her out there this spring. Whereas before I saw only loss, I now believe in hibernation and resuscitation. My waking dream is that all of our surrendered sons and daughters will become our hibernating children . . . newly awakening to the resuscitating power of our mother-love.

@ @ @ @ @ @ @ @

CHAPTER FOUR

Make a Good Noise

Good Noise
Lyrics by John Gorka, 1994

Tell me the truth what are you living for
Tell me why, why are you near
Cause if you cannot make yourself a good noise
Then tell me what you're doing here

Now we all got the hand for the gimme
We all got the mouth for the much obliged
But when it comes down to giving back
We give the eye to the other guy

Oh it seems that so much trouble
Is simply caused by the angry word
Although silence can be a virtue
I say it's a good noise that's preferred

Now you've got every right and reason
To be down in the dumps today
Aren't you just adding to the problem
If you've got nothing good to say

Sure there are wars, disease, injustice
Rich men walking on your hands
But tell me how can you ever take a breath of hope
Talking down your fellow man

@ *Oxygen Mask* @

Date: May 15 7:25 PM EST
From: ElisaMB@aol.com
To: bmoms@abcd.edu

I am glad Julie listed some of the things that birth mothers can do within the adoption reform movement. There will forever be disagreements about reforming adoption laws and preserving families in this country. Each of us needs to discover what we do best, and how much we can handle at different phases of our healing. Some make great public speakers; others are more comfortable confiding a difficult truth to a trusted friend. Some (like me) prefer to write letters to other members of the adoption triad; others prefer to write to a legislative representative or to a newspaper editor.

But I think the first and most important step is to learn to lead honest lives with ourselves and within our closest circles. Personally, the gradual integration of my two lives has been the greatest healer. It has also had greatest impact on the people with whom I regularly interact.

Many of us, however, are in too much pain to do much more than struggle towards our own healing. It is difficult to help others with their fear, pain, anger, even ignorance, when one is overcome with fright, pain, rage or lack of knowledge. It is like the emergency instructions they give parents on an airplane flight: *First put on your own oxygen mask, then secure one on your child.*

@ *The Birds, the Bees and Relinquishment* @

Date: Dec. 16 12:57 PM EDT
From: ElisaMB@aol.com
To: Multiple recipients of Triad List

A birth mother asks: «How have all of you dealt with having other children after adoption? How do you explain the adoption of your child to his brothers and sisters?»

Celeste replied: «I didn't want my kids to fear that they'd be relinquished, too. So I waited until my eldest was thirteen. Perhaps that was too long. My middle child was nine at the time, and he took it all in stride. Perhaps pre-adolescence is a better age for such revelations. Of course, it could all just be a matter of personality . . .»

It is truly horrible to look into any one of my daughters' eyes, and to realize that this could have been the child I lost! It is difficult to avoid the pain of one child's absence from my life as I enjoy the presence of my subsequent children.

Each of my daughters has come to see their older brother's adoption from the private perspective of "There, but for the grace of God, go I . . ." A birth mother's subsequent children do eventually realize that it could have just as easily been they who ended up adopted and raised separately from their original mother, father, and siblings.

I became a birth mother before I became a mother. Thus, it was not until after I had given birth three or four times that I began to grapple with how and when to talk to my children about sex, babies, and the surrender of their brother. I made two important decisions. I decided to search for my son until I found him. Secondly, I would try to explain his relinquishment to each of my daughters as soon as they could possibly comprehend it.

I could and did honestly tell my subsequent children how much I regret my decision to relinquish their older brother. Ultimately and ironically, it is my regrets over my decision, rather than any attempts to justify it, which in turn substantiate my love for and to my subsequent children. I don't spend all my time crying over spilled milk. But when they ask me those soul-searching questions, I can tell them how deeply it hurts me. They see how much I miss my son. And I can acknowledge their pain and their loss as well.

I have often worried about how the adoptive parents of my son have explained his adoption to him. The agency social worker told me that by age five, the adopted child should definitely be told that he or she is "adopted." But what does "adopted" mean to a five-year-old mind?

At five or six years of age, my daughters each began to ask questions about having babies. The rule of thumb I have used in explaining the birds, the bees, and relinquishment to them, was to limit these discussions to:

1. Briefly stating a simple fact such as, "All babies have one mother and one father."
2. Waiting for the child's response, which is usually a question.
3. Asking the child as many questions as I needed, in order to make sure that I understood her.
4. Answering that specific question alone.

The wisdom behind this formula is that it allows the child to take control of the discussion. She is told only what she is capable of comprehending, at her own pace and depth. This has worked out well with each of my daughters throughout their pre-school, pre-adolescent and teenage years. By the kinds of questions they ask, I can usually tell how much they understand versus how much they are ready to hear.

The most difficult part for me to explain to my daughters, both factually and emotionally, is how and why their half-brother has a different father. Of course, had my husband also been Jacob's father, his relinquishment may have been even harder for both of us to explain to our daughters. But whatever the particular truths and circumstances of a relinquishment, it is best for our children to hear it first from their parents.

@ *Coercion* @

Date: Dec. 10 4:47 PM EDT
From: Mimi@aol.com
To: Multiple recipients of Triad List

Very few of us adoptive parents considered that the other parents of our children were coerced to surrender them for adoption. December is the month when Amy's original mom Mary was banished to St. Anne's, a home for unwed mothers. I want to share my thoughts about coercion with you now.

I am fifty years old. When I was growing up, there were two options for anyone who got pregnant before marriage: adoption or a shotgun wedding. Simple: two options, based mostly on the reaction of your parents or of your boyfriend's parents. I didn't view that as coercion, which of course it was. I knew that if I or any of my friends got pregnant, it was off to Father Baker's at Our Lady of Victory. I didn't even know what an abortion was until nursing school. Abortion was never an option. When the topic came up, after saying we would never get pregnant, 90% of us would add, "Why, I would go to Father Baker's, of course, and place my baby for adoption." Saying, "I would keep the baby" was not in the realm of possibility.

In nursing school our dorms were near another maternity home. Sometimes we nursing students would be in the same little shops near the hospital with the girls from the maternity home. I must confess to you that we did not have kind attitudes toward them. We were quite the smug, self-righteous student nurses. If we were out walking and they were out walking, we would be sure to cross to the other side of the street because we did not want any passersby to think that we were one of THEM. I look back now and I am ashamed to admit this, but I had no shame back then. I accepted society's judgment of unwed mothers.

Jump ahead now to the 1970s. My husband is sterile, and we discuss whether we want children. We decide we do. We had always discussed adoption, even if we became biological parents. But when push comes to shove, do we really want to adopt? *James decides we should look into artificial insemination first, so we go to hotshot infertility doctors and are accepted into the program. I go for the first insemination and as soon as we get to the car, I start bawling. Emotionally, I simply could not accept being inseminated with another man's sperm. It felt like adultery. And how could I someday explain to my child, "I don't know who your father is . . ."? I did not get pregnant from that insemination, and I never returned for another.

So we adopt. I have shared how our first child is from South America. We apply to Catholic Family Services. Because Catholics are a 1% minority in our part of the country, there was a need for Catholic adoptive families. The only prerequisites were that our infertility be documented, and that we live more than fifty miles from the agency. I thought, "Wow, this is great! No long wait!" This was in 1978. Not once did I consider that these babies were being coerced away from their original moms. Since abortion was now legal, and since many single moms were keeping their babies, I thought that these young women were making hard but loving decisions. I felt very lucky to adopt a second baby when I had friends in other parts of the country still waiting to adopt their first child.

In May of 1979, Amy is born; by August of 1979, we have our new daughter. I do not think about her birth mother much. When we went to the agency to pick up our baby daughter, I remember hoping that Amy's mother was sitting in a car watching to see who would go in without a baby, and come out carrying one. I wanted her to know at least what we looked like. For years, I had this fantasy that she was watching us that day. At each follow-up visit with the agency, I would ask how Amy's birth mom was doing. I always got the pat reply, delivered as only nuns can do: "She's fine." Twice, after the adoption was finalized in court, I wrote to the agency to ask if the birth mom had contacted them to find out about her daughter. Both times I was told no, that birth moms seldom return to the agencies asking for information. When Amy was about four years old, she wanted to know her birth name. I had asked for it at time of placement but was not given it. This time when I wrote, I was given her first two names: Anne Elizabeth.

Now move ahead to 1995. I still never once thought that Amy's birth mom had been coerced to give her up for adoption. I join America On-line. I read birth moms' accounts about how they were coerced by their families and by society. I had already read Carol Schaefer's *The Other Mother*, so I was beginning to understand that, what I had accepted as "the way it was," was really coercion. I began to understand that many birth moms had the decision made for them. But I had no need to worry, because Amy was placed in 1979. Amy's birth mom could have kept her baby, if she had wanted to.

Now it is July of 1995. I am sitting in Amy's birth grandparent's living room. Amy's birth mother Mary is dead.

The parents shared with me the story of Mary's pregnancy. Mary had gone on a class trip to Washington, D.C. She calls home, hysterical. They can make no sense of what she is saying. She returns home earlier than scheduled, and appears to them to be a changed person. But they ask not one question! Their daughter, who had been vivacious and outgoing, is now withdrawn. She is gaining weight. Finally, she tells them, "I was raped on that school trip to D.C." Perhaps Mary had been given chloral hydrate, or perhaps she had disassociated, as happens in trauma.

Mary's parents take her to the parish priest, who immediately sends them to the agency which is working with us. A few days later, Mary is sent to an out-of-state maternity home. She is sixteen years old. It is almost Christmas. How alone and scared she must have felt! She gave birth the following May, returned home, and was sent to confession. What was Mary supposed to say in the confessional? "Forgive me, Father, for I was raped . . ."?

Mary was expected to go on as if nothing had happened. She never again spoke to her parents about her pregnancy, about her baby, about her stay at St. Anne's. Her younger siblings were not told about her baby until they were adults. Her aunts, uncles, and cousins were not told until after I had searched for and found Amy's birth family.

Was Mary coerced, or did she make a difficult but loving decision, as I had always believed? Of course she was coerced! I knew it immediately, as I sat in that living room listening to her parents.

This has been very hard for me to acknowledge. I would rather go on believing that Mary freely made her decision, but I cannot deny reality. Her decision was made by her upper-middle-class parents, and by her parish priest, and by nuns. By a celibate male who probably felt that Mary had no right to make her own decisions. By nuns whose very religious order was established in large part to provide maternity services.

Peace, Amy's adoptive mom

@ *Open Letter to Adoptive Parents* @

Posted on America Online by ElisaMB@aol.com

Just as you realize that not all adoptive parents adopt for the same reasons or motivations, not all birth parents relinquish for the same reasons. You may feel that it behooves each adoptive parent to try to understand the very different reasons for adoption, as well as the dissimilarities in the ways the children are raised, and to which degree each particular set of adoptive parents chooses any openness within that adoption.

Do you, as an adoptive parent, make a distinction between the parents who adopt international children and those who adopt domestic children? Between the adoption of an infant and the adoption of an older child? Between the adoption of a healthy child and the adoption of a disabled child? Between the adoption of an orphan and that of a child with living relatives? Is it considered any more acceptable within the adoption community, or within your own heart, to adopt a child whose original parents truly abandoned that child, or who truly chose to relinquish their parenting rights?

Regarding the greater community of birth parents, my answer to those questions is a resounding yes.

What do all adoptive parents have in common, regardless of how or why or what kind of child they've adopted? It is the fact that you have each assumed the legal and moral obligations to raise a child to whom you did not give birth. By the same token, the single commonality linking each original parent of an adoptee to any other birth parent is the fact that we have each legally relinquished those same obligations.

Beyond those two statements, however, there remains very little common ground between many birth parents. I can list three very important distinctions:

1. *Coercion:* The birth parent who was psychologically or physically coerced to surrender a child for adoption made his or her "choice" or decision or "adoption plan" based on an entirely different set of assumptions from those of the birth parent who was not coerced.

2. *Choice:* The birth parent who chose to relinquish his or her parenting rights to a known set of parents, within the system of open adoption, also based that decision on an entirely different set of assumptions than the birth parent who surrendered a child to an unknown set of parents.

3. *Motivation:* I know that this will sound simplistic and highly judgmental. But I do not care to be grouped in the same category with a mother who insists that she gave informed consent to relinquish her newborn baby. It is particularly distressing to be linked together with parents who relinquish their newborn specifically *because* of the baby's disabilities. This is a sore point for me, as I found out after the fact that I had relinquished a child with "special needs." Had I been made aware of my infant's disabilities, placing him for adoption would no longer have been a consideration.

@ *Denial and Healing* @

Date: May 12 1:01 PM EST
From: ElisaMB@aol.com
To: Alicia@aol.com

Alicia writes: «We must look to one another (and to others in the Triad) for inspiration in our "recovery" from what has been a painful journey for each of us, because no one else really understands the loss.»

Before I had ever befriended or even met another birth mother, my grief was understood by at least one other person who had no direct connection to adoption loss. My dear mentor, colleague and friend Joy had simultaneously experienced the death of an infant daughter and of her mother, several years before she hired me to teach with her. It was my first job out of college; my baby was less than a year old. Even after the birth of her twin sons, Joy's bereavement was as raw as my own. Her empathy was immediate and genuine.

With very little need for enlightenment, many others can empathize with our loss. The families of MIAs, of kidnapped children, of real handicapped survivors; our own spouses and subsequent children. Any of these individuals, especially if they are further along in their own journeys towards healing, can understand us better than a triad individual who is still in denial.

Alicia writes: «Their denial is allowing them to gather psychic and emotional strength and, when it is sufficient, they will emerge, ready for their own "hero's journey," as Betty Jean Lifton puts it so eloquently.»

I hope that you and Betty Jean are right. But my personal conclusion is that the longer and deeper the denial, the less likely one is ever to truly emerge, or to embark on any pathway to healing.

Alicia writes: «I agree with your timebomb theory. But, I also believe in honoring and accepting each birth mother where she is on her personal path before her inner bomb explodes. Someday she will need our "recovered birth mothers'" honest appraisal of the State of Adoption and Birthmotherhood and our support and inspiration for survival.

But it is so important to let each one be where she is now, because someday she will need to trust that we accept her. (If you remember, trust is a big issue for us birth moms.) I wholly believe it is not a gift to a birth mother in denial to "out" her, insisting she be aware of something further along her path than she is able to see. That she trigger her timebomb before she is ready. A gentle warning from us, perhaps; an intrusive insistence that she see clearly right now, no.

I firmly believe we cannot judge for any birth mother where her feelings lie or when her timebomb will detonate. I do believe we can love each one, let her find her way, and, when she's out of denial and in pain, offer her support and a clear view of adoption issues that affect her. That is why support groups, on-line and off-line, are so vital.»

I agree with you, Alicia, that it is always best for people to ask for it before they get it, and that we should then dole it out in gentle doses, like waiting for our children to ask questions about sex.

But I do not believe it is possible to "trigger a birth mother's timebomb before she is ready." Denial is the powerful safety mechanism which keeps this from happening. The timebomb can only be detonated by the birth mother herself, and only when she deems herself "ready."

@ *Cat's Lament: An Adoptee Speaks Out* @

Date: Sept. 16 6:49 EST
From: Cat@aol.com
To: ElisaMB@aol.com

You know me pretty well by now, Elisa. I make no effort to appease or to avoid hurting another's feelings, if their opinions will invalidate the pain which adoption has caused me and other adoptees I have known. I think relinquishment is the single most selfish thing a woman can do, especially if the woman clings to fantasies about what it is really like to be adopted.

I feel it completely possible for a biological mother to never have your timebomb occurrence, but let me explain why. It is human and natural to suddenly realize the consequences of choices one has made in one's life, but there are ways to avoid that realization.

I am an adoptee who has found her birth mother. *Linda has managed to remove herself emotionally enough that she is neither able to listen to, nor to comprehend the problems I have had as a result of being adopted. My birth mother was disappointed to find out that my life has not been a fairy tale. She dealt with it by denying that I have had a hard life. The children she kept won't talk to me, because they are jealous of the supposed perfect life I had. I can't put into words the terrible hurt I feel in some way, each day, related to being put up for adoption . . . hurt that is not acknowledged by Linda, because it will ruin her idea of having "done the right thing."

Birth mothers somehow feel they have made the "superior" choice by not having an abortion. But they think they have only given up a baby, instead of a real-life human person for whom a happy adoptive home cannot be guaranteed. And even if the adoptive home is a good one, the baby-child-teen-adult will have an individual personality which is affected by the mere fact of being adopted. I believe that adoption and abortion are both bad. With abortion, however, the woman makes a choice and carries that guilt forever. She is completely responsible, and people are angered by it. With adoption, a woman makes a choice, gives away the guilt, takes no responsibility for the child's entire life, then gets patted on the back for it.

Regardless of their circumstances (romantic, financial, etc.) birth mothers need to realize that their children are likely to feel betrayed, abandoned, worthless, and unloved. Adoptive parents do not make up for the original fact of being unwanted. Explanations after the fact will never be able to even slightly reduce the feelings of absolute rejection and abandonment for which the word "adoption" is a screen. Regardless of the reasons for relinquishment, the more likely questions will be: Why did you keep the other children, and not me? Why didn't you search for me, or try to regain custody? Was I just not worth fighting for?

Privacy on the part of the birth mother seriously borders on selfishness, however it may dressed up as "wanting the best for the child." Confidentiality means she does not have to feel guilty if the child does not have the best adoptive home, as she does not have to know about it. Privacy also protects the adoptive parents, and pretty much allows them to treat the child any way they wish.

I am offended by women who, under the umbrella of adoption, try to paint themselves as loving and caring, while insisting that their right to privacy does not contradict that. I only have sympathy for the mothers who truly never wanted to relinquish, who have missed their child, and who try to reunite.

blessings, Cat

@ *Abortion and Adoption* @

Date: July 13 12:15 PM EDT
From: ElisaMB@aol.com
To: bmoms@abcd.edu

An adoptee who has experienced abortion writes: «I think the work we do in adoption reform needs to cover issues like money, and to change social atmosphere to where the man's obligation and responsibility are called upon, and not relieved by options such as adoption or abortion.»

In my mind, there are more similarities than there are differences between the long-term effects of either adoption or abortion, for the birth mother in particular, but also for the adoptee. There is no more choice in abortion than there is in adoption. There is a part of every mother, whether she chooses to have an abortion or to surrender her baby for adoption, which perishes. A woman with an unplanned and unsupported pregnancy must choose between:
a.) her own life and her child's life
b.) her partner and her child
c.) two or more of her children's lives.

Birth mothers have unequivocally stated that adoption aborts motherhood every bit as much as abortion precludes it. Both choices are irrevocable and irreversible. They each cause the unnatural, physical and emotional severance of the natural unity between mother and child.

@ *The Question*
Birth Mothers Were Not Asked @

Date: Sept. 21 8:08 AM EDT
From: ElisaMB@aol.com
To: bmoms@abcd.edu

A birth mother wrote: «I would not discourage adoption as an option for someone pregnant with a child they feel unable to care for, for whatever reasons. I would, however, want to make them more aware, beforehand, of what will lie ahead. I had no idea. I still have no idea. I am still learning (the hard way) not to encourage or discourage an unwed mother-to-be to do anything other than what she really wants to do.»

The problem is that her counselors, doctors, social workers, family and friends rarely if ever stop to ask her that most important question: "What do YOU want for yourself and for your baby?" A majority of pregnant women, regardless of their age, marital, physical, financial, social, or emotional status at the time, if asked that question, would truthfully reply: "I want to be the best mother I can be to my child."

That question needs to be put to any expectant mother at least three times:
1.) when she is deciding whether or not to have an abortion
2.) prior to the birth of her child, and
3.) after the baby is born but before she signs its life away.

She rarely gets asked that question because most people are not willing to give her the kind of help she would need in order to be the best mother she can be to her child. And I'm just talking about her innermost circle of family and friends, not about the social work world at large. When it comes to establishing social and legal policy, the general public (my own teenage daughters included) and tax-payer is afraid that, by helping such a needy mother and child to stay together, they would be establishing very bad precedents for the future. They fear that teenagers would go out in droves, get pregnant on purpose, drop out of school, and become welfare mothers forever. That is like saying that all women intend to use abortion as a means of birth-control.

I am convinced that you and I and many other women would not have given up our children had our family members put such a question to us directly. But families and friends and social workers and doctors and clergymen and lawyers are always going off behind closed doors to confer about what is best for poor so-and-so. Poor so-and-so is the one who has to live for the rest of her with all of the consequences of that decision, not the others. This scenario is being repeated with adult adoptees who are denied their birth records. It comes down to adults being treated like children by people who have no right to act as their parents. It is a form of playing God with another person's life.

A child who has conceived a child is no longer a child. He or she may not have "earned the right," legally or otherwise, to be treated with all the respect that one adult generally accords another. But that teenager has crossed a line over which he or she can never fully cross back again. They will never be able to reclaim or to continue their childhood in quite the same way.

Teenage mothers and fathers deserve all the help, support, and guidance available from all those who claim to love them. There have been centuries of human culture and social history, and there exist societies more civilized than ours today, where teenage parenthood and teenage marriages are the norm. Accepted and supported as such, teenage parenthood can be every bit as successful as any other kind of family unit.

@ *In Whose Best Interest?* @

Date: Sept. 27, 18:35 EDT
To: bmoms@abcd.edu
From: ElisaMB@aol.com

An open adoption birth mother writes: «As far as honorable open adoptions are concerned, I would have to say that it can be considered honorable if it is an educated, informed decision, without coercion; if the birth parents have chosen the adoptive parents and if the adoptive and birth parents have mutual respect and trust for each other.»

I remember the first time that a very embittered birth mother told me that, if her teenage daughter were to get pregnant, she would tell her to definitely abort the baby before she would ever tell her to put the baby up for adoption. I disagree with her, but I understood exactly what she was saying. I should ask that birth mother whether, given this definition of an "honorable open adoption," she would now advise her daughter any differently.

The question of an "honorable adoption" will always hinge on the individual mother's answer to the question: "What would be in my child's best interests?" That answer will reflect not only the mother's ethical, philosophical, psychological and religious beliefs, but also the particular circumstances surrounding her pregnancy.

Just as we could not predict our surrendered child's future, neither can any woman faced with making that decision today predict its outcome. Nor does she have the time to wait and see what the studies will reveal about the best interests of the child.

I agree that we all need to learn more about open adoption and about its long-term effects on each of the triad members.

But I think we also need to ask ourselves: What is the ultimate goal of this education? Is it to promote open adoption as a facile solution to the proven evils of the archaic system? Is it simply to provide another option for the woman considering aborting her child? Or is it in order to find out in whose best interest this, or any form of adoption, really exists?

Ask any birth mother or any adult adoptee: "Do you feel that the adoption has resulted in your best interests?"

I await and earnestly hope for the day when the majority of openly-adopted adults will emphatically declare: "The adoption was in my own best interests!"

@ *Single Motherhood in Germany* @

Date: Sept. 19 9:15 AM EDT
From: Magda@uni.Germany
To: ElisaMB@aol.com

I'm getting more and more annoyed at our society. A great deal of problems could be resolved if there were more nurseries at universities, schools, companies, and in residential areas, where a mother could leave her child from early morning until early evening. Shops are closed at night and are open only one Saturday afternoon per month.

Here in Germany, a working mother or father of a minor child is entitled to an additional paid leave of ten days if the child is sick. This policy is hard to enforce, however. Many women are reluctant to claim their rights. Therefore, I believe that it would be better to have a "sick-room" adjoined to the nursery. The nursery system is not very popular in Germany and hardly available yet.

A common practice in Germany now is for single mothers, even those who graduated from university, to live off social welfare and their additional $450 monthly "mother's allowance." (Married mothers receive the same amount. Working mothers are the only women who don't receive it).

I prefer the nursery system, because that way a mother can still continue her studies or work and earn money. And she is not directly dependent on the tax payers' money or at his mercy. It is not too expensive; a state would not collapse. Some practices are better in the U.S.A.; some are better in Germany.

Magda

@ *Twenty-Six-Year-Old Memories* @

Date: April 1 5:52 PM PT
From: Joan@aol.com
To: ElisaMB@aol.com

Every time I reveal my status as a birth mother, I always get back an adoption-related story. Yesterday was another example.

I was home from the office by noon, as I was waiting for the window cleaning couple and, best of all, my daughter Karly was on her way from Los Angeles for a visit. I was running around like crazy, picking up and cleaning (always a sign in my house that company is on the way!) and chatting with the cleaners. I told the window lady that I was waiting for my twenty-six-year-old daughter. I explained that I had not raised her, but that I now felt so fortunate to have her in my life.

When I had finished speaking, I didn't expect much of a response. (I just know they will think something along the lines of, "I raised mine, what's wrong with you?" But I'm always wrong). There was about half-a-minute of silence, and then she said that she was the mother of a twenty-six-year-old adopted daughter!

Her daughter very much w ants to find her birth parents, and the window mom wants to help with the search. An attempt some time ago revealed that all records had been lost and so they gave up, but not permanently. (An adoption agency was involved, but the window mom went directly to the hospital to pick up her daughter. She was adamant that no one else hold the baby.)

She said she vividly remembers all the details and emotions of that day, as clearly as if it were yesterday. I said that I also vividly remember that day. She and I could not be further apart in what we felt on that day, twenty-six years ago: I lost a daughter and she gained one. But I sensed she really understood.

Hugs, Joan.

@ *Birthfathers Have Secrets, Too* @

Date: March 21 6:26 PM PT
From: Joan@aol.com
To: ElisaMB@aol.com

It's funny how when something is going on in your life, all of a sudden you see it everywhere. If you are pregnant, all you see at the mall are pregnant ladies. When you are at the mall with an infant in the stroller, no one is pregnant any more; they all have infants in strollers. If you buy a purple car with yellow stripes, no doubt you'll see six more next week.

And so it is with me, now that I am involved in adoption. (Correction: I have been involved for twenty-five years, but I have barely acknowledged that until now.) Now that I am reunited, and interacting regularly on the Internet mailing lists and forums, I am finding adoption all around me in "real life."

Most of these experiences take place at lunch with an old or new friend. Today's example happened with a person who is working with us part-time. *Marnie is married to one of our full-time employees.

We were talking about babies and birth because my lunch partner is pregnant. When Marnie told me her age, I told her that I have a daughter who is only three years younger than herself, and so the story came out.

Before getting married, Marnie had struggled as a single mother for seven years. I thought that she would be quite critical of me. I am always waiting for someone to ask, "How could you have done such a thing?" As usual, I remain my own, and perhaps my only, judge and jury. It turns out that Marnie and I both got pregnant the first time, with our first boyfriends.

Her own adoption-related story was actually her husband's. *Sam is the birth father of an eight-year-old boy, and he didn't find out until after the adoption placement. He knows the first name, and had photos for a year, then nothing. It is an open adoption to some degree, but Sam is not involved. It really surprised me when Marnie said that, to this day, no one except for her (and now me), knows about Sam's son, not even Sam's parents. I have never thought much about a birth father having his own secrets, his own separate life that is not to be talked about.

The birth father of my daughter never knew about her, so I never had occasion to think about how he might be reacting on her birthday, when he sees a same-age child, when he has subsequent children, when he gets up every day, for that matter. If he were to find out that he has a daughter, how would that be incorporated into his own life? What kind of impact would it have?

Karly isn't searching for her birth father, so for now I will be in the wondering stages. I am probably much more curious than Karly is, to see him. I would like to see if she resembles him, and to know if she has any other siblings, and what they are like. But that is 100% Karly's decision and so for now, it rests. And that's O.K., too.

Joan

@ *Out of the Birth Mother Closet* @

Date: Sept. 25 1:37 PM EDT
From: Judy@uvm.edu
To: Multiple recipients of Triad list

Hello all, Tonight I face a challenge in a class I am taking. The assignment is to do a five- or ten-minute 'culture watch' presentation, and I automatically chose birth mothers. Writing the paper was a breeze, but now that the day for the presentation has come, I'm trying to hold myself together.

My stomach is doing flip flops. I'm trying to summon all my inner strength. I am frankly scared to death at the thought of facing these twenty faces, and being judged by them. I keep sliding back into the spot of a shameful seventeen-year-old girl, instead of a woman who has come full circle. I need to get a grip!

All advice is welcome. I need to chase this fear away and to get centered before I attempt this 'coming out.'

Thanks, Judy in Vermont

Date: Sept. 26 12:33 PM EDT
From: Judy@uvm.edu
To: Multiple recipients of Triad List

Yesterday I posted about needing strength and help to make it through my class presentation on 'birth mothers' and about the lifelong ramifications of adoption on our lives. I was petrified, and you gave me strength.

It was as hard as I thought it would be. The pain from the past twenty-seven years was not to be hidden. It surfaced, despite my insistence that it stay hidden, for the entire class to see as I sat before them. I do not like to cry publicly, yet my tears were good for them to see: a "real birth mother" still dealing with the pain and losses. My fear of facing my emotions in front of them was not enough to stop me from presenting this important information about how adoption arrested our emotions and split us from our true selves. I will not be an impostor any longer. This talk was necessary as part of my healing journey to regain my lost self.

They say it gets easier the more we confront the demons that haunt us, and hopefully that's true. This whole event was physically exhausting yet fulfilling. I am still feeling the effects today.

Judy in Vermont

@ *The Only One* @

Date: Sept. 3 2:32 PM EST
From: ElisaMB@aol.com
To: bmoms@abcd.edu

During my search for my son, I came across an ad in the C.U.B. newsletter. Joanne was seeking another birth mother who had relinquished a child through the same small Christian adoption agency in northern New Jersey. I immediately replied to Joanne's message and we began a long and supportive correspondence which continued over the next four years. Our "search buddy" system culminated with each of us locating our children at the same time.

Although Joanne and I had relinquished our children six years apart, we were able to compare notes. Dozens of letters, telephone calls and visits had been ignored by the same social workers. Joanne, too, was another "only one." I had recently been to the agency for my "postpartum visit" a few years after Joanne's first visit. I had been told: "Oh, Elisa, we are so sorry that your decision has caused you such pain over the years. But, my dear, you are the only birth mother who has ever come back to tell us so."

Sometimes I wonder whether the saddest lies come after it is too late, or before.

@ *The Best Adoption Whorehouse in America* @

Date: Nov. 3, 11:14 AM EST
From: ElisaMB@aol.com
To: Alicia@aol.com

Dear Alicia: In honor of my daughter Suzanne's birthday, I have composed the following letter. Please forward this reply to the Director of Post-Adoption Services at The Gladney Center, whose article you have just published in *Adoption Triad Forum*.

Ever since I received the first of numerous Edna Gladney Foundation full-color brochures propagandizing your services to prospective birth parents, I recoil at the very mention of that name. I was working as a volunteer counselor in Boston when that glossy brochure arrived addressed to our non-profit organization. The idea was for me, the volunteer counselor, to recommend this alluring maternity luxury resort in Fort Worth, Texas, to any woman faced with an unplanned pregnancy. I would immediately dial the Edna Gladney toll-free number in Texas and then suggest to my unfortunate pregnant client that she hop on the next plane from Boston to Texas. I could tell my client that she wouldn't have to pay for her plane ticket, or to worry about housing or medical costs; that Edna Gladney would find the most wonderful (and need we add well-heeled) adoptive parents for her baby; that she could even swim and play tennis while awaiting the birth of her unplanned child! And now, twenty years later, I see that if my client's relinquished child wanted to know who gave birth to him or her in that maternity wonderland, a team of Gladney Post Adoption Service's social workers would help to make the correct match.

I actually did pick up the phone at the Birthright office that day, and spoke to several people at Edna Gladney. I do not recall the details of that conversation, but I do remember tearing up the pamphlets and dumping them in the Birthright trash can. It was clear enough, even to me, even way back then, that The Edna Gladney Foundation of Fort Worth, Texas was nothing less than the Best Big Adoption Whorehouse in America!

My husband and I decided to move our young family from Boston back to our original City of Brotherly Love. There was a Birthright office in Philadelphia, too, but I decided to discontinue my volunteer crisis pregnancy counseling. At least I would never have to look at another Edna Gladney brochure.

But why, ironically, did I now begin to hear that ubiquitous name, again and again? It seemed that everywhere I turned in the blue-blooded and moneyed Streets of Philadelphia, I was faced with yet another set of adoptive parents parading around their beautiful blue-eyed, golden-haired child, whom they had miraculously adopted through The Edna Gladney Center in Fort Worth, Texas!

What "Post-Adoption Services" do you provide for the birth mother who is seeking her child? What do you say to her when she comes back to you, begging for a photograph, a kindergarten story, or an invitation to her child's high school graduation? What do you tell her if her child's adoptive home-life did not turn out to be the fairy-tale story which you or Edna or whoever, promised to her during those long months of pre-surrender, all-expenses-paid housing, prenatal care and counseling? What if her child never comes back to the agency to find her? What if all the adoptee wants is his or her medical records? What if the adoptive parents have given their adopted *Wunderkind* to understand that seeking out his or her birth parents would be a most ungracious thing to do?

This "policy that will work and is sensitive to all members of the adoption triad," which your distinguished Board of Directors has devised, what does it do for the birth parents and adoptees who have yet to realize that they may have been coerced into an unnecessary and irrevocable separation from one another at birth? Edna Gladney remains today, as it was then, the intermediary to that fate!

In the past year alone, through my Internet connections, I have met a dozen women, from all over the United States, who relinquished their newborns through Edna Gladney. All but one of these mothers has no idea whether her son or daughter is dead or alive. The other mother recently discovered that her son is dead. She had waited for him to turn eighteen before attempting to locate him. He had committed suicide one month prior to that eighteenth birthday.

I applaud your good intentions to begin, at long last, to rectify some of the injustices of your system of adoptive placement. But I submit to you that, until you have "devised a policy that will work" to prevent any further unnecessary separation of mothers from their newborns, The Gladney Center will only be perpetuating the devious practices which it has always carried out to such perfection.

Sincerely yours, Elisa M. Barton, Philadelphia, PA.

@ *Elephant in the Living Room* @

Date: Oct. 2 11:30 AM EDT
From: ElisaMB@aol.com
To: Multiple recipients of Triad List

On the first anniversary of her surrendered son's suicide, a newly bereaved Edna Gladney birth mother writes: «There was no surprise party!»

There was no surprise baby shower, either. Remember that disappointment? But just the other day, my mother surprised me with a belated gift of honesty. My mother, who rarely cries, sobbingly explained to me: "Elisa, you know that for the last nineteen years I have always called you on July 26th. And I never said a word; I just called you. That is all I could do, but I did it every year."

I replied to my mother: "Playing the make-believe game with the very person who attended the birth of my firstborn baby only added insult to injury for me. But even if it has taken you nineteen years, you've said it now, and that makes all the difference."

We each develop different coping mechanisms. Avoidance seems to be a popular choice. Some of us feel dishonest unless we declare: "There's an elephant in the living room!" And we feel betrayed by those who just don't want to talk about it.

@ *Firetruck in the Living Room* @

Date: Oct. 2, 1995 1:07 PM EDT
From: Joan@aol.com
To: Multiple recipients of Triad list

Dear Elisa and all,

Your mom's honesty was indeed a great gift and hopefully it will open the door for more. Even though your mother skirted the issue every July 26th, she did know it was his birthday, and she was thinking of you.

I made it real clear to my parents that I didn't want to talk about it ever again. But I wish they had been able to show me that it didn't have to be that way. When I told my mother that I had found Karly, she asked me, "How old is she now?" and "When is her birthday?"

Ten years after surrendering my baby, I mentioned my daughter to my sister for the first time. She didn't even know that the baby was a girl, or whether I had known my child's gender. Talk about ignoring the elephants, they were all over the place.

In group therapy a while back, our elephant analogy was a firetruck that came crashing through the wall. My firetruck hit when I became pregnant. My parents and I absolutely refused to believe that it was there, for seven months. Finally, we acknowledged that it was there, but we tiptoed very carefully around it. We didn't know what to do with this firetruck. We didn't know how to take care of it. We didn't know that other families had firetrucks, and that it was normal to talk about the fact that a firetruck had come jamming through the wall and had stopped right in the middle of the living room. We did what we thought we were supposed to do: we thought that if we ignored it, it would go away. We just kept pretending it wasn't there. Then we pretended that we had forgotten all about it.

Some twenty-six years later, the truck has been cleaned, tuned up, repainted and, for the most part, removed. But I know there will always be a residue.

Hugs to everybody, Joan

@ *Christopher's Story* @

Date: 30 April 19:51 PST
To: Multiple recipients of Triad list
From: *Christopher@crl.com

The last year has been somewhat difficult for me, since I have begun trying in earnest to deal with some of the issues and emotions related to my adoption which I have long left deeply buried. Your voices in particular have helped me to begin to understand my birth mother's situation.

My name is Christopher, and I am a forty-six-year-old adoptee. I was born September 20, 1948 in Tennessee. I now live in California with my wife and two children. This note contains almost all that I know about the circumstances of my birth and adoption.

In 1948 *James and *Frieda *Worth lived on *Covered Wagon Road in Tennessee. Their neighbors on either side both had adopted children, and were visited frequently by Mrs. Minnie Brock of the Tennessee Children's Home Society. During one of her visits, Mrs. Brock was looking for a home for a young girl during her pregnancy. She discussed this with Frieda Worth, whom she had met through the neighbors.

At the time, Mrs. Worth had four other children, including two-year-old twins, and was also pregnant. She offered the girl a home in exchange for some help with the children. The girl who came to live with them was my mother.

*Andrea Smith was a pretty girl of eighteen in 1948. Her family lived somewhere along the Tennessee-North Carolina border. My father said he saw her once, and that she had beautiful red hair, which Mrs. Worth confirmed. She had to quit school early, in the eighth grade. Her family had been unable to afford schoolbooks, which were not provided in Tennessee then. Andrea had been working as a waitress in Maryville, Tennessee when she became pregnant. She visited with Mrs. Worth's sister in Maryland once with the family, and was described as rather quiet, a "very nice young lady."

After Andrea's baby (I) was born, she went back to her family. The Worths heard from her only once more, a letter thanking them for their help.

In 1988, my adoptive mother told me about Andrea's stay with the Worth family. This was quite a surprise to me, as the baby Mrs. Worth had been carrying had become a good friend of mine; we had attended grade school together. I wrote to Mrs. Worth, and received a letter containing much of the above information. It was Mrs. Worth's belief that Andrea's family had known nothing of her situation, believing that she was working out of town. Andrea had told the Worths that her baby's father was a student at the University of Tennessee in Knoxville. Mrs. Worth felt that my birth father also knew nothing of the pregnancy. Andrea had never mentioned his name.

Mrs. Worth wrote that, at that time in Tennessee, mothers who were giving their babies up for adoption were not allowed to see them at all. When Andrea came home from the hospital, she was very distressed by this. She cried for several days, for just one look at me, just to once hold me in her arms.

For reasons I do not understand, I was sent from the hospital where I was born to another Catholic hospital in Knoxville, Tennessee. I was there for about six weeks, before my adoptive parents could pick me up. My mother tells me that I didn't cry, or make any other sound, during the two-hour trip in the car back to their home. Given my propensity for wordiness and for general noisiness, I cannot help but wonder at that.

My adoption was finalized on October 26th, 1949, in the County Court of Sullivan County, Tennessee. I have the original decree of adoption. The blank for the name of the baby had the name "Douglas Frank Smith" typed in, but this was then erased and replaced with an 'X.' My original name can still be read through a magnifying glass. My birth certificate number is 141–84957. I also have much of the original correspondence between my adoptive parents and the Tennessee Children's Home Society, as well as copies of all my correspondence with the Tennessee Department of Human Services.

Despite the fact the I was adopted through the now-infamous Tennessee Children's Home Society, I don't believe that my adoption was one of the suspect ones. That may be wishful thinking on my part. I will most likely never know, until I find Andrea. This fact was, however, responsible for a strange event that occurred two years ago.

One evening, I received a call from Florence Fisher, the founder of ALMA (Adoptees Liberation Movement Association). Ms. Fisher asked me if I would be interested in help with my search. I had been registered with ALMA for several years. Thus, it seemed to me that, if they could help me, it would have already happened. But I said I was interested anyway. She said that someone else would be calling me shortly. The person who called was a representative of the Oprah Winfrey show. He wanted to find Andrea, and to have us reunite on the show. While the offer of help was attractive, I declined it. I did not think that it was appropriate. How would Andrea feel about being publicly reunited with a son about whom no one else knew? I did not want to meet her for the first time on television. Our parting was relatively private, and I would like for our reunion to be private as well.

My thoughts and emotions about my relinquishment and adoption have run the gamut from anger and depression to acceptance and happiness. But I think most of the bad feelings have burned themselves out. I am no longer angry at anyone, except at the current system of adoption and closed records. I just want to get on with my life, and with my search.

I will find Andrea someday, if only to tell her that things have worked out well for me. And that she has two wonderful grandchildren. And that I hope that she doesn't feel too badly about what happened. I pray that, someday, my original mother and I will be able to tell one another our own stories. And that she will still have that longing to see me, and to hold me in her arms. Thank you for listening.

Christopher

@ *The Electric Kool-Aid Adoption Test* @

Date: May 7 5:11 PM EST
From: ElisaMB@aol.com
To: Multiple recipients of Triad List

Christopher, I would have gone on *Oprah*. I would be delighted to receive a call from Florence Fisher. My daughters, who are more like you (reserved and reasonable) than they are like me (obnoxious), have nevertheless promised that they will go on the air with me, if Oprah ever calls. (We draw the line at Geraldo, even though I think he is Cuban.) But Christopher, if you were to call those guys back, and to give them your go-ahead, I hereby offer to come and meet your birth mother beforehand, to show her your beautiful letters, and to reassure her that she is not alone.

Christopher's story, and the fact that he and I are going about pursuing our reunions in such a diametrically opposed fashion, reminds me that we can and will achieve the goal of eradicating the unnecessary separation of infants from their mothers in this country. The only part of my "birth mother life" which doesn't literally sicken me is the marvelous difference in style and communication between each of us. When I look at the adoption reform movement as a whole, I see a delightful neon-colored rainbow coalition: Electric Kool-Adoption-Aid! The acid test is whether we can eventually combine the best of those unique qualities to make a difference.

Our very own rock'n'rollin' birth mother Maria has an Adoption-Aid benefit concert in mind . . . perhaps as a reunion celebration between mother and son guitarists?

Over New Year's, a friend of mine was invited to appear on CBS *This Morning*. *Louise is an adoptee and a talented private investigator who had recently reunited a mother and daughter via her efforts on the Internet. The two adoptees were convinced that the mother, who had never met another birth mother, would hate the idea. The younger ladies hemmed and hawed with the television people. But the birth mother just said, "Hey, how come nobody asked me? I'll go!" And she did. All the way from California to New York. Louise flew in from Colorado; the adopted daughter came from Iowa.

Louise asked me to please meet the three of them in Manhattan for the taping. She was nervous about her first appearance on national television, and she also wanted me to support the birth mother from California. I took a magnum of champagne and my two teenagers to Manhattan with me.

We had quite a party in Louise's hotel room. The two grown adoptees were jittery wrecks. The birth mother breezed right along, obviously enjoying herself.

All three of the ladies put on a great show. After the taping, the reunited mother and daughter got to celebrate the new year as well as their new life together, in Manhattan. They spent three days, all alone together for the first time, and partially on CBS' tab.

My own older daughters also got to meet their first "other mothers." They came away from that weekend understanding their crazy mother, and the crazy world of adoption, a lot better.

@ *La Cocotte-Minute* @

Date: May 9 8:52 AM EST
From: ElisaMB@aol.com
To: Joan@aol.com

100 mg. and you still don't feel any better? I would be a fool and a hypocrite to say something like "just give it time" or "be patient." Sometimes it takes more energy to be patient, than it does to do something, to do anything. I think you have learned this the hard way already, during all those years you suffered in silence. I just don't know what to say to you anymore about the continued failure of anti-depressant drugs or psychotherapy, or reunion, to "cure" you. I honestly feel that it is all that repressed grief, anger, hurt, loneliness, and love (!) which continues to cause you the greatest harm.

Think of it this way: you have a firetruck-load of intense feelings, all bottled up inside of you, like in a pressure cooker. They are like one huge ugly boil, getting ready to explode. It hurts like hell just before it pops. Your pressure cooker began to whine a long time ago. It's too late now to just open it up all of a sudden. It would explode all over you, and you'd get burnt even worse that way. Your kitchen ceiling would be a real mess to clean up (and I know what a cleanliness-fanatic you are!) If the cocotte-minute analogy comes anywhere close to your reality, it should follow to take the following steps:

What to do with a burnt pressure cooker:
1. Turn off the source of the heat. 2. Wait for the whining to dissipate. 3. Loosen the cover just slightly, once it has cooled off. 4. Take the cover off completely and let out the steam. 5. Throw out what is inside the pot. 6. Throw out the pressure cooker, too. 7. Buy yourself a new pot. 8. Find yourself a new recipe 9. Try out the new recipe in the new *cocotte-minute*. 10. Taste it to see if it's any good, adding more spices as needed.

@ *A New Question from an Old Friend* @

Date: May 4 8:47 AM EST
From: ElisaMB@aol.com
To: multiple recipients of Triad list

A wonderful thing happened yesterday. An old friend asked me a new question. Ann's sincere and gentle question was:

"Elisa, did you ever feel forced or pressured to place the baby for adoption?"

That is not entirely a new question for me or for many of you, but it blew my mind coming from my friend Ann. For ten years now, Ann and I have prayed together, played bridge and golf together, even traveled to Germany together. She is one of the two close friends who accompanied me to visit the father of my son a few years ago. Ann was also our daughters' pediatrician for several years. We met one another during the period of my search for my son. We have had long and intimate discussions about everything under the sun, moon and stars. While we rarely agree on anything, we have generally felt comfortable enough with one another to voice those differences.

As we all know, however, there are certain subjects which one learns to skirt or to avoid for the sake of maintaining harmony with our closest friends, with our spouses, with our children and with other loved ones. The subject of "biological parents" searching for their legally relinquished children was one of those issues which I had learned to avoid discussing with Ann. We had agreed to disagree. But there were numerous times when this issue threatened to terminate our long-standing friendship altogether. It had generated a distancing between us over recent months. The last time Ann and I had had one of our heart-to-hearts, I had mentioned the subject of my book. She had cut me off, saying, "I don't want to hear about it. You know how I feel about biological parents searching for adoptees."

That conversation took place in my kitchen about five months ago. I had not spoken to Ann since. Yesterday, I had an appointment with my eye-doctor, whose office is around the corner from Ann's house. I decided to drop by for an impromptu visit.

Just moments after the usual catch-up, Ann said she had seen "that movie about the birth mother finding her son" on TV last month. I waited for her to go on, expecting her to return to her theme of disgust over this subject. Instead, she asked me that question. I immediately knew that Carol Schaefer's story had touched my friend's heart in a new and special way. Ann's question meant that she was finally ready to hear what it is like to be the "Other Mother;" why I had needed to search for my son when I did; and why I still desire an honest relationship with him.

I answered Ann's question very briefly, explaining the subtleties of coercion in surrender. I am looking forward, with a wonderful sense of hope, to unlocking another door in our stunted friendship. I know now that Ann is ready to listen without pouncing.

For the first time in over a year, we are playing golf together next Wednesday. Ann is very good and I am very bad. I expect that, after the second or third hole, she will ask me another good question, to which I will sincerely reply. But wish me luck anyway.

@ *Everybirthparent* @

Date: Nov. 5, 11:45 AM EST
From: ElisaMB@aol.com
To: Adoption Triad Mailing List

The public confessions of Oprah Winfrey, Joni Mitchell, Jonathan Edwards, and Roseanne Barr notwithstanding, there remains a huge dearth of true publicity about the real-life, Everyman Birth Parent. I do not wish to imply that it is easier for a celebrity to come out of the closet as a birth parent than it is for us regular folk. But it is equally imperative for the rest of us to make our presence known to our unique communities-at-large.

Old friends and family members presumably already know, trust and respect us for what and who we are as "non-birth parents." Allowing these everyday people in our everyday lives to also see our birth-parental dimension is a huge step in the direction of dispelling the many ugly myths and false images which continue to plague birth parents in the eyes of an otherwise ignorant but general public.

"Birth parent bashing" goes on everywhere one turns: through Dear Abby or her twin sister Ann Landers' column; on your local or nationally televised news program; in the Movie-of-the-Week; in the courtroom; in fiction and non-fiction books; on the church podium; on the Internet!

Imagine what is going on in the minds of our very children, of their schoolteachers and friends. Or in the minds of our very spouses, and of our colleagues at work. If the only birth parents they ever read about or hear about or see represented in a movie are surrogates or prostitutes or thieves selling their babies for money, or dumping their newborns in the nearest trash barrel, or "stalking" their relocated children, or trying to "kidnap" their legally relinquished children, then what are they supposed to think about the rest of us? Can we really blame them, or blame the rest of the general public, for assuming that every birth parent is similarly motivated? I too am guilty of ascribing ugly and evil motives to other birth parents.

One solution to my dilemma has been to try to counter that public image by baring my private one. It's been amazing to see how many "coincidental" occasions arise, in the course of any single day. The subject of birth parents is everywhere around me, on a regular basis. One recent but typical example:

A bright and cheery neighborhood mother, highly active and respected in our local church and school community, calls me on the telephone. Barbara and I have taught together in the same Sunday school as well as in the same local public school system. She is organizing the volunteer ushers for an upcoming international women's tennis tournament and is calling to recruit me. She asks how I have been, how my teaching is going this semester, how the girls and my husband are doing. I say to Barbara, "Great, but busy. Good busy, not bad busy . . . I'm working on a book." She inquires about the subject of my writing. I tell her that I recently discovered how to operate a modem, and that I became an e-mail junkie. I tell her about the Internet mailing lists . . . Finally I tell her that the book is about what it feels like to be a birth parent.

Without a moment's hesitation, Barbara tells me the story of one of her closest friends from college, a birth mother who was recently reunited with her relinquished twin daughters. In twenty-one years, her friend had never let on that she was a birth mother, to Barbara or to anyone. The twin daughters had just searched for and found their birth mother. I am now the second birth mother whom Barbara has "met"!

Our telephone conversation continues to surprise me. Barbara jots down the titles of several books about birth parents and about reunions, which I recommend for her friend to read. I keep expecting Barbara to come up with an excuse to quickly hang up the phone. But she wants to hear more about how and why I became a birth mother, and about my relinquished son. She is fascinated to learn about this entire "other life" of mine. Unlike that of her close friend, my birth mother story has never been a deep secret. But to Barbara, it is a somewhat shocking revelation.

Barbara is neither a journalist nor a gossip. I do not expect to have people in church, at school, at the local supermarket, or at the tennis tournament this week approaching me to say, "So, Elisa . . . I hear you gave up a baby for adoption." I do expect, however, that I have planted a seed, however tiny, which will eventually blossom into a wildflower of truth, growth and understanding, about who Everybirthparent really is.